T0114082

Praise for *Shamanism Made Easy*

"Within minutes of meeting Christa Mackinnon, I knew she was the real deal and that she was some incarnation or embodiment of ancient knowledge here to inspire healing and transformation in all of those she works with. Christa's book Shamanism Made Easy *was like medicine to me and as soon as I had it in my hands I could feel my soul being replenished and supported. I believe in Christa and her mission; her loving attention to ethics, sustainability and making a difference is an inspiration to the world. May Christa's sacred work enrich your life."*

KYLE GRAY, BESTSELLING AUTHOR OF *RAISE YOUR VIBRATION, ANGEL PRAYERS* AND *LIGHT WARRIOR*

"This book is essential reading for beginners, but also very interesting for people like me who have walked for a long time on the path of shamanism. I love the way in which Christa explains the fundamentals of shamanism but also gives psychological and scientific perspectives on what is happening in your brain while you practice. For people new to shamanism, you will find many techniques to begin your shamanic practices, and experienced people like me will find beneficial explanations from somebody that has been combining psychotherapy with shamanism in an amazing way in her practice and her life."

SERGIO MAGAÑA, AUTHOR OF *THE TOLTEC SECRET* AND *CAVES OF POWER*

"This book is a must for anyone who wishes to explore shamanism and understand how it can be used in modern day life. Written by a highly experienced modern-day Medicine Woman and inspiring shamanic teacher, it is easy to read, clear, authentic and informative. I particularly love the practical ideas suggested and have included them in my own work. A book I return to again and again."

VANESSA TUCKER, AUTHOR OF *THE ART OF YOU* AND FOUNDER OF 'WALK YOUR TALK RETREATS'

"Any wise seeker, particularly one who wants to explore the vast inner and outer realms of expanded consciousness, needs an experienced and ethical guide they can trust. Christa Mackinnon stands out as one of them and Shamanism Made Easy *is the perfect guidebook for those taking their first steps into the great mystery that waits for us all."*

Matthew J. Pallamary, author of *The Center of the Universe Is Right Between Your Eyes* and *Spirit Matters*

SHAMANISM
Made Easy

❖ Also in the Made Easy series ❖

The Akashic Records

Animal Communication

Astrology

Chakras

Connecting with the Angels

Connecting with the Fairies

Crystals

Discovering Your Past Lives

Energy Healing

Feng Shui

Goddess Wisdom

Lucid Dreaming

Meditation

Mediumship

Mindfulness

NLP

Numerology

Qabalah

Reiki

Self-Hypnosis

Tantra

Tarot

Wicca

SHAMANISM

Made Easy

Awaken and Develop the Shamanic Force Within

CHRISTA MACKINNON

HAY HOUSE
Carlsbad, California • New York City
London • Sydney • New Delhi

Published in the United Kingdom by:
Hay House UK Ltd, The Sixth Floor, Watson House,
54 Baker Street, London W1U 7BU
Tel: +44 (0)20 3927 7290; Fax: +44 (0)20 3927 7291
www.hayhouse.co.uk

Published in the United States of America by:
Hay House Inc., PO Box 5100, Carlsbad, CA 92018-5100
Tel: (1) 760 431 7695 or (800) 654 5126
Fax: (1) 760 431 6948 or (800) 650 5115; www.hayhouse.com

Published in Australia by:
Hay House Australia Ltd, 18/36 Ralph St, Alexandria NSW 2015
Tel: (61) 2 9669 4299; Fax: (61) 2 9669 4144; www.hayhouse.com.au

Published in India by:
Hay House Publishers India, Muskaan Complex, Plot No.3, B-2,
Vasant Kunj, New Delhi 110 070
Tel: (91) 11 4176 1620; Fax: (91) 11 4176 1630; www.hayhouse.co.in

A catalogue record for this book is available from the British Library.

This book was previously published under the title *Shamanism* (*Hay House Basics* series); ISBN: 978-1-78180-587-9.

ISBN: 978-1-4019-6846-5
E-book ISBN: 978-1-78817-279-0

Interior images: Isabel Bryna Mariposa Galáctica

At the center of the universe dwells the Great Spirit. And that center is everywhere. It is within each of us.

BLACK ELK: BLACK ELK SPEAKS

Contents

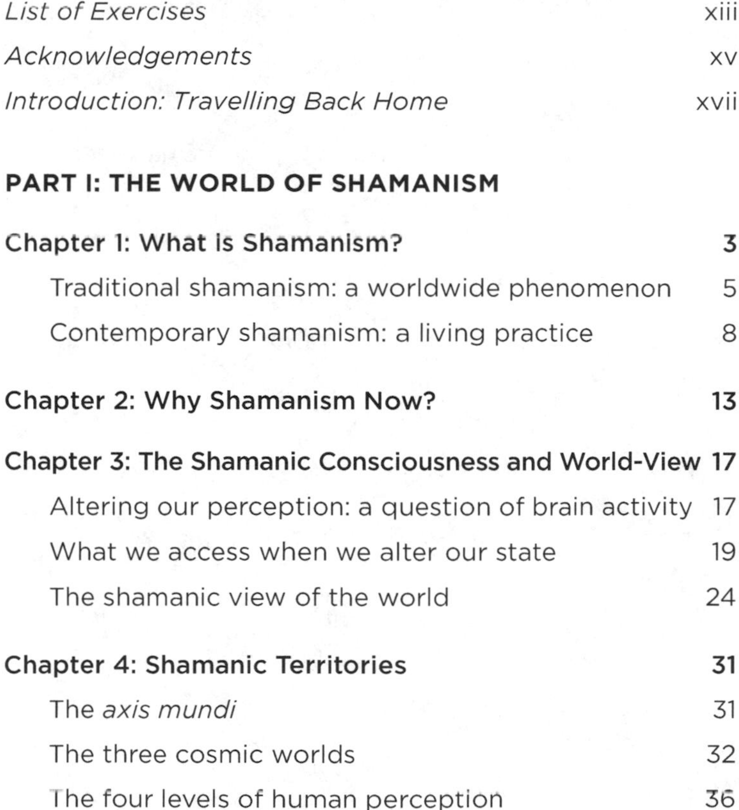

List of Exercises xiii

Acknowledgements xv

Introduction: Travelling Back Home xvii

PART I: THE WORLD OF SHAMANISM

Chapter 1: What is Shamanism? 3

Traditional shamanism: a worldwide phenomenon 5

Contemporary shamanism: a living practice 8

Chapter 2: Why Shamanism Now? 13

Chapter 3: The Shamanic Consciousness and World-View 17

Altering our perception: a question of brain activity 17

What we access when we alter our state 19

The shamanic view of the world 24

Chapter 4: Shamanic Territories 31

The *axis mundi* 31

The three cosmic worlds 32

The four levels of human perception 36

PART II: AWAKENING THE SHAMANIC FORCE WITHIN

Chapter 5: Bringing the Shamanic Dimension into Your Daily Life **41**

Basic skills and tools 42

Working with spirit: calling the spirit forces 46

A sense of the sacred: create an altar and clear your space 48

Find a daily ritual to connect with spirit 53

Embodying energy in matter: power objects 56

Chapter 6: The Shamanic Journey **61**

Establish your place of power 64

Connect with your spirit allies: power animals of the lower world 66

Connect with your spirit allies: upper-world teachers and guides 71

Chapter 7: Psycho-Spiritual Work Between the Worlds **75**

Transformative journeys: retrieving, releasing, healing, developing 77

How to integrate your journeys 85

Chapter 8: The Power and Beauty of Ceremony and Ritual **89**

Traditional ceremonies and rituals 90

How ceremony works its magic 92

How to create your own ceremonies 94

Chapter 9: Dancing with Spirit **105**
Traditional trance dance 106
Contemporary adaptations: dance yourself awake and free 108

Chapter 10: The Medicine Wheel **115**
The powers of the four directions 116
The human aspects of the wheel 119
The circle and the diagonals 122

Chapter 11: Spirit, Soul and the Sacred in Nature **125**
An Earth-based traditional cosmology 125
The starving of our sacred Earth souls 129
Contemporary shamanic nature work and tools 130
Reconnect with the sacred in nature and your own nature 131

PART III: THE WIDER WEB OF LIFE

Chapter 12: Embedded in the Cycle of Life **141**
Creation stories: the power of formation myths 141
Expand your sense of self: find your own creation myth 143
Widen your circle: connect with ancestors and descendants 146
Death as part of life: the gifts we receive when facing death 151
Working with death in shamanism 154

Chapter 13: Sacred Medicine Plants **161**

Traditional plant ceremonies 162

The sacred plants: ibogaine, San Pedro, peyote, mushrooms and ayahuasca 165

A word of caution and encouragement 172

Chapter 14: Shamanic Work in the Dreamworld **175**

Normal dreaming and sharing 178

Intentional dreams and lucid dreams 179

Conclusion: The Dreamer and the Dream 185

References and Notes 189

Further Reading 201

Index 205

About the Author 215

List of Exercises

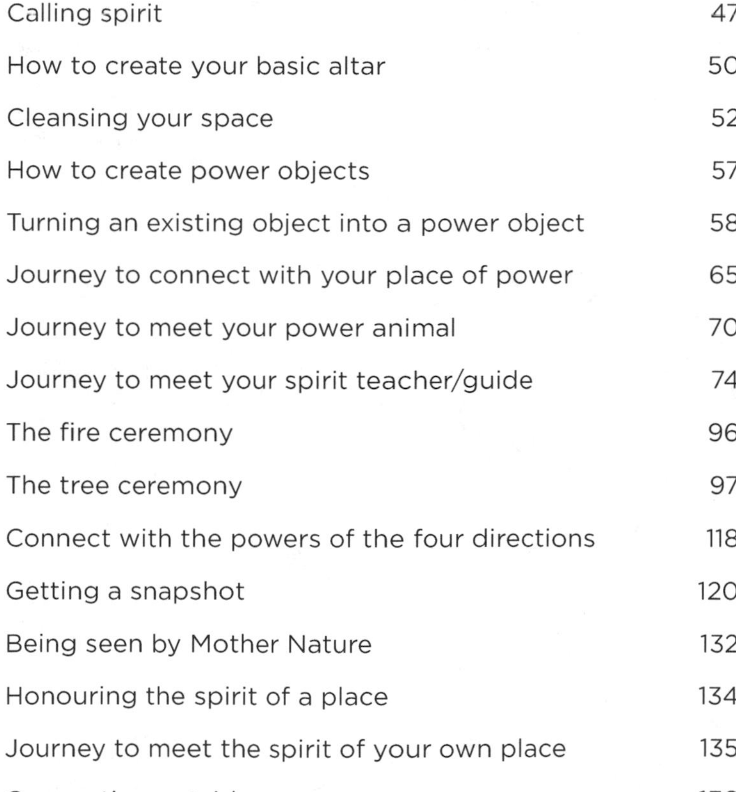

Calling spirit 47

How to create your basic altar 50

Cleansing your space 52

How to create power objects 57

Turning an existing object into a power object 58

Journey to connect with your place of power 65

Journey to meet your power animal 70

Journey to meet your spirit teacher/guide 74

The fire ceremony 96

The tree ceremony 97

Connect with the powers of the four directions 118

Getting a snapshot 120

Being seen by Mother Nature 132

Honouring the spirit of a place 134

Journey to meet the spirit of your own place 135

Connecting outside 136

Connecting via the shamanic journey 137
A connecting awareness walk 137
'Let something find you' walk 138
Finding your own creation story 145
Journey to connect with an ancestral guide 148
Journey to connect with a descendant 150
Journey to explore the realm after death 157
Journey to become familiar with your own physical death 158
Dancing your last journey 158

Acknowledgements

Like everybody who is interested in shamanism, I am greatly indebted to the indigenous people around the world who have - often against all odds - kept their ancient practices and teachings alive and are sharing them with us.

My heartfelt gratitude goes to all the teachers, students, clients, colleagues, friends and 'fellow dreamers' who have walked with me on my path. Writing about this subject would have been impossible without their input over many years.

Appreciation is due to the truly amazing Hay House team, particularly to Michelle Pilley, Amy Kiberd, Julie Oughton, Polina Norina and Lucy Buckroyd, and to my editor, Lizzie Henry, whose immense professionalism and skill made the editing process not only a pleasurable one, but also an invaluable learning experience.

Special thanks to Matthew Pallamary, shamanic explorer, writer and friend, for letting me reprint the experiences he describes in his book Spirit Matters, to Joanna Pine for giving me permission to use her first 'trance dance experience', which set her on the path to shamanism, and to all the clients and students who allowed me to share their stories in this book.

Finally, as always, I thank my husband, David, and my daughter, Kamala, for their support and encouragement, and especially for 'loving me just the way I am'.

Introduction

Travelling Back Home

A friend who knew that I had been on a spiritual path for many years before becoming involved in shamanism once asked me, 'Why shamanism?' And, whilst giving her all kinds of explanations, I suddenly remembered the intense experience I had had during my first shamanic workshop, which I can best describe as the ecstatic feeling of a weary traveller who finally comes home. During that first workshop, something deep inside me woke up and I remembered how it felt when we still gathered around fires in the evenings, beating drums and telling stories, living lives that were infused by the mystical and sacred, a time when we were still deeply connected to nature, community, soul and spirit.

Having walked a fairly eclectic shamanic path now for many years, I am convinced that what I experienced during that first workshop – and the deep impact it had on my life – explains why we have seen an immense revival of shamanism and, over the last few decades, an unprecedented development of contemporary varieties worldwide. What I experienced at that time is what we now call 'the surfacing of the shamanic archetype into consciousness', a kind of inherited memory pattern held within the collective unconscious and within each of us. Such patterns, which are also sometimes referred to as 'the shaman within' and which exist already within each of us in potential form, are coming to the fore now because what they represent is needed in the world and because the time is right.

Shamanism is an umbrella term for both the most ancient spiritual traditions known on this planet and the many contemporary varieties. Traditional shamanism was our tribal ancestors' way of exploring and working with the forces around them, including the energetic 'other' worlds and spirit forces. The shaman, the 'one who knows', formed the bridge between these energetic worlds and the material world of the manifested realms, working in alignment with the wishes of spirit for the benefit of the community and its individual members. To this day, shamans are healers, ceremonialists, visionaries, psychics, dreamers, manifestors, divinatory practitioners, psychopomps and more.

For me, shamanism was the last step on my spiritual journey. I had always been interested in human consciousness and knew from an early age that there was much more to reality than what we normally experience.

My early journey led me to travel the world, which opened my eyes and heart. I was drawn to Eastern spirituality, lived for some time in the Osho ashram in India, which was greatly liberating, and later became involved in Buddhist practices. During those times I had my first, very frightening, 'shamanic calling', which brought me to the brink of death and which I only much later defined as a dismemberment experience, which is well known as an initiation practice in traditional shamanism. This experience, together with my meditation practices and some out-of-body experiences and visions, brought about by my use of psychedelic substances, changed me profoundly. I knew without any doubt that there were underlying realities that were energetic in nature, that consciousness could travel and that life was eternal.

After going to university to study psychology, I became a therapist specializing in trauma and then a university lecturer and trainer. The big adventures of my youth and early adulthood became pleasant memories as I lived a well-ordered life as a successful professional, a wife and a mother. Still, somewhere deep within me there was a longing, a hole, which my by now reduced spiritual practices, my quite fulfilling career, my social activities and even my love for my partner and daughter failed to fill.

It was at this stage in my life that I participated in my first shamanic workshop. This proved to be a turning-point. Over the following years, I became more deeply involved in shamanic teachings and practices. I attended workshops and training courses at home and in the USA with many well-known teachers in the contemporary field, and later I learned from and worked with indigenous shamans from Peru, Ecuador, Brazil and Mexico. Still, I was a reluctant shamanic apprentice. I could not say that shamanism had failed to enrich my life considerably or that I was not attracted to the immense variety of approaches and tools it offered. My reluctance was due to the realization that the deeper I delved, the more I understood that my work as a psychologist, therapist and trainer had to shift. Shamanism could not be something that was merely a part of my life: I was being asked to make it my life's path.

There was much that I loved about shamanism in those early days. I loved that it brought the sacred back into my life and provided me with the means of experiencing the many layers of my reality – inner as well as outer. I loved the fact that it was dynamic and experiential, free of any religious connotations, and that most shamanic practices were conducted in altered states of consciousness. I enjoyed the work with the many forms of spirit and loved learning to experience and work with energies. I also enjoyed exploring the enormous variety of shamanic tools and practices, ranging from journeying, meditating, drumming and dancing to vision quests, nature work and ceremony, lucid dreaming, medicine wheel teachings, sweat lodges and psychedelic medicine plants, to name just a few.

Nevertheless, I continued to separate my 'serious' work as a psychologist and therapist from my shamanic development. This changed only when I spent some time in Ecuador, learning from an indigenous shaman. During that time I had a dream that provoked the only critical remarks I ever heard from him, along the lines of: 'The dream shows that shamanism is in your blood. But you still refuse to be what you are meant to be. You have a choice: you take your innate power or you die slowly.'

After that I began to run shamanic workshops and training courses for laypeople and then, finally, integrated shamanic teachings into my therapeutic work with private clients and my various training courses with professionals, developing my own style of working in the process, to the immense benefit of hundreds of clients and students.

Incorporating shamanism into my professional life was a big step in the right direction, but it took another wake-up call, a dark night of the soul when I went through heartache I had not imagined possible, before I was able to take stock of my life honestly. All my defences broke down and, shaken to the core, I ended up in hospital with heart failure. At that point I had to decide what was important and what was not. Crucially, I felt very strongly that if I didn't get my priorities right and complete the work I had been put here to do, I might as well leave this planet.

During my healing process I resigned my post as the course director of a large hypnotherapy institute, stopped working as a psychologist and began to write about ancient wisdom traditions and their incorporation into contemporary therapy. I ran more shamanic courses for therapists and spoke at conferences, trying to make professionals understand that as long as we refused to cater for the human soul, we were not serving our clients. My first book, *Shamanism and Spirituality in Therapeutic Practice* (Jessica Kingsley Publishers, 2012), pioneering the subject a few years later, was a result of this work.

I have never looked back. Now I feel more whole than I have ever felt before. I know my path, my calling and the life I want to lead – connected to spirit, to the shamanic community and to my own deeper self. I am able to tune in and out of underlying fields and use the powers and help we can find there to create a life that is in tune with my deeper self. I trust that shamanism will continue to help me in the process of becoming 'all that I can be' in this life by offering exactly what I need, and I trust that I will be able to go with the process instead of resisting it.

Trying to define precisely what shamanism did for me – and what it can do for you – is not easy, but looking back at my own journey and at those of the many hundreds of people with whom I have worked, I can honestly say that it can do 'everything' for you. It can certainly enrich your life, open worlds and enchant you. It can bring the sacred back into your life and enable you to become whole. It can help you to find meaning and purpose and expand your consciousness.

As this book will show, shamanism connects you to your Earth roots whilst helping you to branch out into the sky. It reconnects you to the lineage of humanity, starting with your ancestors and descendants and embedding you in a circle that loves you dearly. It also helps you to communicate with spirit, access spirit help and live your life in harmony with your own spirit essence.

As shamanism consists of a vast field of teachings, knowledge and practices, I have structured this book based upon what has worked for me and for the many people who have attended my workshops and courses over the last 15 years. I have also selected mostly practices that you can use by yourself, omitting or just touching on those that need training, such as, for example, soul retrieval, deep energetic healing and healing with herbs and plants. Part I presents an overview of shamanism, Part II gives you a wide range of tools for your own healing and development, and Part III offers some more advanced teachings, practices and tools, though not all of them lend themselves to being tried at home. I advise you to go through the book in chronological order, because the exercises build on one other, leading you deeper into shamanism and into yourself.

Once you follow the shamanic path, teachers and opportunities come your way naturally. So I invite you to get started and, as you embark on this journey, I assure you that the worlds you will find, the spirit help you will access and the healing you will experience will change your life.

Part I

THE WORLD OF SHAMANISM

'Not only is the shamanic type emerging in our society, but also the shamanic dimension of the psyche itself.'

THOMAS BERRY, *THE GREAT WORK*

Chapter 1

What is Shamanism?

Shamanism is the oldest known spiritual practice and discipline. Like all organically developed systems, it is an evolving tradition: it has taken a range of forms in various cultures at different times. However, it is also a universal path, showing remarkable similarities across the globe and across time.

We find traces of shamanism in the Americas, Russia, Africa, Asia, the Far East and China, as well as in Europe, Australia and New Zealand. We have 30–40,000-year-old cave paintings in Spain and France. We have cave paintings stretching back about 28,000 years in the outback of Australia. The rock art of Niger in Africa dates back 30,000 years and a skeleton of a female shaman found in Israel is about 12,000 years old. Ancient myths, stories and traditional ceremonies also contribute to our knowledge about shamanism. Strong elements of shamanic spirituality are found in Celtic and Russian myths, the creation stories of the Americas, Australia and Africa, and the ceremonies, symbols and beliefs of Buddhism, Taoism and Shintoism.

The continuum of this ancient spiritual path has been disrupted, broken and suppressed many times, mainly through conquerors, missionaries and political activities, but, astonishingly, it has never been fully eradicated. In very remote areas, lineages of shamans have kept the tradition alive through the ages; in other parts of the world, it has been forced underground, only to surface once more as the suppressing forces have retreated or loosened their grip. We can see this in South America, especially in the Amazon and the High Andes, where shamanism still flourishes, despite forceful attempts by Spanish invaders and missionaries to suppress it. The same applies to Africa and Australia, where tribal shamanic customs were never fully eradicated, despite the efforts of colonial and religious powers. The endurance of this ancient spiritual practice can also be seen in the revival of the North American indigenous traditions, as well as the vibrant post-Soviet resurgence of shamanism in Siberia and Mongolia, which I saw with astonishment on a recent trip.

Most sources indicate that the word 'shaman' stems from the Evenki language of the Tungus tribe in Siberia, as it is closely related to their word *saman*, which can be roughly translated as 'one who knows' or 'one who is excited, moved, raised'.[1] The gender-neutral term 'shaman' is now used in general for people who are involved in the tradition, even if they have different titles in different cultures, such as medicine man or woman in North America and Canada, healer in Africa, or *kupua* in Hawaii.

Traditional shamanism: a worldwide phenomenon

Historical accounts

Our knowledge about shamanism in indigenous cultures is incomplete, but besides the artefacts and myths, we have accounts from early European visitors[2] to different parts of the world, as well as contemporary academic studies.[3] Lately, some accounts have come from shamans around the world who are descended from traditional lineages.

The accounts from the early Europeans encountering tribal shamans, starting around the 16th century, are important records, as they have negatively influenced popular thinking about shamanism for centuries, and to an extent still do. For the Europeans, the ecstatic rituals, magical ceremonies, peculiar healing practices, unfamiliar chants, masks and ritual clothing, beating of drums, trance dances and bizarre visions produced much fear and horror. Their descriptions reflected that fear and also the Christian religious views of the times, as they equated shamanic practices with witchcraft and consorting with the devil. Later, during the Age of Enlightenment, in accordance with the new 'rational thinking', most Europeans accused shamans of being either tricksters and charlatans or psychotics and schizophrenics.

It was a long time before the western view of shamans began to change. A more positive picture only began to emerge between 1930 and 1950, when anthropologists ethnologists, psychologists and biologists embarked on studying the remaining indigenous cultures around the world more intensely, learning their languages, interviewing shamans and recording their own investigations. In 1932, for instance, John Neihardt recorded the still famous life story of Black Elk, a medicine man of the Oglala Sioux, revealing him as a great visionary, healer and leader,[4] and in 1949 Claude Lévi-Strauss, the renowned French anthropologist, likened shamans to psychoanalysts, stressing their immense knowledge of the human mind and finally laying to rest the opinion that they were deranged or mentally ill.[5] Most importantly, anthropological reports showed that despite their cultural differences, all shamans claimed to communicate with spirits in the interest of their community.

Nevertheless, it was not until the second half of the twentieth century that shamanism received the credit it deserved. Mircea Eliade's *Shamanism: Archaic Techniques of Ecstasy*, published in 1951 and still a major reference work today, provided a synthesis of cross-cultural research whilst eliminating many misconceptions and prejudices and coining the term 'masters of ecstasy' to describe the shamans' altered states and soul flights to other worlds.

Whilst Eliade's book inspired professionals, it was Carlos Castaneda's 1969 book *The Teachings of Don Juan: A Yaqui Way of Knowledge*[6] that ignited unprecedented popular interest and motivated Western spiritual seekers and researchers alike to live with indigenous people, 'study' the shamans and partake in (mainly plant-induced) ceremonies and quests. The subsequent reports showed that shamans worked as psycho-spiritual and physical healers, ritualists, mythologists, mediums and visionaries, using their skills for the benefit of their tribes, and were pioneers in exploring the wider capacity of the human mind.[7]

Characteristics of traditional shamanism

These and other studies have shown that traditional shamans worldwide, without being a culturally homogenous group, have certain cosmologies, ways of working and characteristics in common.

Traditional shamanism is a path universally used to expand consciousness to connect with energetic other worlds and to work with those forces for the benefit, health and harmony of a community and its members. Shamans are therefore seen as intermediaries between worlds and guardians of the spiritual, psychic and ecological equilibrium of both the group and its individual members.

Shamans within indigenous communities are interdependent with nature, with the spirit worlds and with their tribes. This interdependence is the trademark of indigenous traditional shamans, who either come from a lineage or are 'chosen by spirit'. Their training is long and intense and during their initiation they often go through a period of transformation accompanied by a life-threatening mental and physical illness, which leads them through death and rebirth experiences in extreme altered states of consciousness.

Traditional shamans had – and still have – vast knowledge about the natural and spirit worlds which forms the basis of their work as healers, visionaries, divinatory practitioners, ritualists and ceremonialists, mythologists, mediums, dreamers, psychics, psychopomps, creators, manifestors and teachers.

In order to 'fly' to the spirit worlds, to work within them and to bridge the worlds, they use a compendium of skills and means. These include smoke and herbs, rituals and ceremony, power tools and clothing, trance dance and trance movements, merging with and shapeshifting into nature spirits and animal spirits, close connections with ancestral spirits and spirit allies, the ingestion of hallucinogenic sacred plants, and the vibrations of drum rhythms, sounds and voices.

Contemporary shamanism: a living practice

Since the first wave of Western interest brought shamanism to wider attention, it has gone through an immense revival and also many changes. It has become part of a progressively more urban, global and technologically interconnected world and attracted countless spiritual seekers and lately growing interest – and acceptance – from anthropologists, medical practitioners, psychologists, physicists, biologists and therapists.

In the early stages of this revival, the 1970s/1980s, many westerners began to bring back what they had learned from indigenous shamans, mainly in South America, and practise shamanism themselves, running courses and workshops and creating schools, centres and foundations.[8] From these schools we now have a second generation of shamanic teachers all over the western world. Traditional shamans and teachers, especially from Mexico and South America, also began to travel to the USA and Europe to spread their teachings, whilst North American elders and teachers from the Hopi, Lakota and Navajo sent increasingly urgent ecological messages to the world, attracting seekers and inspiring foundations, schools and courses.

In the 1990s, African shamanism came to the fore with books such as Luisah Teish's *Carnival of the Spirit*, which introduced the world to the sacred traditions of the Yoruba, and the works of Malidoma Somé concerning the Dagara people.[9]

Over the last 20 years or so shamanism from the Far East and from Tibet and Nepal, which has interesting Buddhist components, has also found its way into mainstream contemporary shamanism. Australian Aboriginal teachers can now be found on social media and at conferences, and in Mongolia and Siberia shamans and their teachings have become accessible and widespread.

Parallel to this, many of the Western shamanic practitioners and teachers have been taking groups of seekers to learn from traditional shamans in various parts of the world and traditional shamans have in turn been opening their doors to an increasing number of people. This has now, especially in Mexico and the Amazon and Andes, almost reached the level of mass tourism.[10]

Adding to the mindboggling diversity, we are currently seeing shamanism being integrated into other movements and disciplines in various ways. The consciousness movement has incorporated shamanic cosmology. Ethno-medicine is growing around the world. Strands of transpersonal psychology have incorporated shamanic views of human consciousness. The ecology movement has very much adopted the Earth-based elements. The interconnection of the modern world is reflected in the mixtures and combinations, the interweaving of the old and the new, that is contemporary shamanism.

Characteristics of contemporary shamanism

It is impossible to define contemporary shamanism precisely, as it is such a mixed bag, but we can, as most literature does, compare it to the traditional and become aware of the similarities and the differences.

Western shamanic practitioners and teachers are not shamans in the traditional sense (I am rather sceptical when they call themselves shamans; I prefer the term 'shamanic practitioner'). They neither come from lineages of shamans nor have they gone through the profound initiation rites and the long training periods of traditional shamans. They are not embedded in classical indigenous communities, with 'place and tradition' grounding their work. In line with developments away from communities and towards the individual, Western shamanic approaches are more focused on the development and healing of the individual.

Nevertheless, contemporary shamanic approaches share their cosmology and many aims and tools with the traditional. They work, as traditional shamans do, towards wholeness, focusing on the integration of the mind/body with the soul/spirit and the whole human with the wider field of spirit. They also work for the community, albeit defining 'community' now in a more global sense or forming communities with a specific focus, such as the many circles that exist locally all over the Western world. They also employ altered states, form a bridge between the worlds, expand our consciousness and help us to understand our own nature whilst bringing us back to a soul-centred way of life, connected to Earth, spirit and the sacred.

Contemporary shamanism is comparable to traditional shamanism in its work with spirits and spirit allies and its use of a vast range of tools that have been developed within traditional shamanism. It uses ceremony, ritual and vibrational instruments, and employs myths, stories and archetypal symbolism, trance dance, vision quests, wilderness camps, lucid dreaming, natural hallucinogens, various energy healing approaches, medicine wheel teachings and more.

Contemporary shamanic practitioners and teachers understand, as traditional shamans do, that the teachings come ultimately from spirit. Good practitioners, although skilled in their craft, will always work with the help of spirit, and good teaching will facilitate spirit connection for the student. In that sense, the teachings and practices developed over millennia belong to us all, as they are derived from Earth and spirit. We can utilize the vast knowledge that is increasingly being passed on to us by traditional shamans for our own healing and development, as long as we understand that shamanism is about spirit, soul, Earth, connection, consciousness and community.

Contemporary shamanism is about experiencing those valuable, timeless and universal teachings and finding our own ways of incorporating them into our lives. As we get involved in shamanic practices, our lives become more enchanted, meaningful, purposeful and authentic, and we take our rightful places as positive co-creators in the developing flow of life, connected to and in harmony with spirit – and our own spirit.

Chapter 2

Why Shamanism Now?

Why is shamanism in all its varieties becoming increasingly popular? Why is this happening now?

In a nutshell we can say that as human beings we have an innate drive to develop into 'all that we can become', and that we have reached a point where a shift in consciousness and a change of our way of life is inevitable if we want to develop further – or even survive – as a species. Our efforts over the last two millennia have focused increasingly on material reality, economic growth, consumption and scientifically orientated mental development. This has produced materially wealthy societies, but has neglected our inner and spiritual development. We have lost our connection to the Earth, to our souls and to the sacred within and without, and are deprived of deeper meaning and purpose. The shamanic archetype, that knowing pattern deep within us, reminds us of how it felt when we were still focused on soul and spirit, embedded in a community and experiencing ourselves as an integral part of existence. It reminds us of what we need to come back to on our human journey if we want to become balanced and whole.

We have reached a point in human evolution where many of us are beginning to wake up to the fact that our materialistic world-views, the economic structures of our societies and our one-sided development have created a range of very disturbing ecological, economic, social and political problems and, most importantly, 'soulless' societies.

The price we have paid is much higher than can be outlined in the context of this book. The environmental devastation, the extinction of species, the destruction and uprooting of almost all indigenous cultures around the world, the cruelty of slavery, the religious crusades, the horrendous world wars and more tell their own story. Even our much-hailed economic progress has now – in global terms – produced an inequality in wealth distribution on a scale never seen before, where 1 per cent of the world's population owns 48 per cent of the world's wealth.[1]

Even in developed countries that have a good share of the created wealth, we still pay a high price. We have reached record levels of so-called 'mental disorders', with depression and anxiety disorders leading the field, and loneliness and isolation following on behind.

The pressure to be 'well adjusted' to a soul-denying society is taking its toll. For me as a psychologist, it is not surprising that the suffering of the soul, which has not been catered for at best and negated at worst in contemporary society for a long time now, is ending up in the consulting rooms of medical practitioners, therapists and psychiatrists in the form of psychosomatic pains, diffuse emotional disturbances, hopelessness, disenchantment and depletion of energy as well as anxiety and depressive disorders.

Jung warned that if we did not explore and nourish the psyche, we would not survive as a civilization.[2] He understood, as many more do now, that we would lose our souls in the process.

The most important understanding we develop when we get involved in shamanism is that there is no 'wholeness', no positive human development, no ultimate joy, contentment and fulfilment, without nourishing our souls, expanding our consciousness and experiencing ourselves as an integrated part of the whole.

So the shamanic archetype within the human psyche is stirring, because it represents what we have lost: the connection to the Earth, to nature, to our soul and to the sacred. It represents all that our fragmented psyche longs for. It represents mystery, magic, community. It represents our yearning to break down the limiting cognitive and ego barriers of our minds, to alter our states and to let our consciousness soar, so that we can experience the sacred in all its awe-inspiring ways. It represents the human quest of going beyond the limits of the ordinary and of experiencing the magical. It represents our power to dream our own life into being.

As you are reading this book, the 'shamanic within you' has already awakened and is asking to be given time and space to develop, so that your journey can unfold.

It is time to begin.

Chapter 3

The Shamanic Consciousness and World-View

To understand shamanism it is important to remember that shamanic work, whether contemporary or traditional, forms a bridge between energetic other realms and manifest reality. Much of the psycho-spiritual work of shamanism therefore relies on accessing those deeper realms and the beneficial forces within them. This requires altering our perception.

Altering our perception: a question of brain activity

There is nothing strange or magical about altering our perception – it is a natural function of the brain. All it requires is a shift away from the type of brain activity that dominates when we are awake and focused on perceiving and processing input from our environment. It can be a mild shift, such as when we daydream, meditate or create, or it can be profound, such as when our brain perceives a serious threat and goes into survival mode, or when we dream at night, or have a near-death experience (NDE).

Basic altered states of perception can be measured with electroencephalography (EEG), which gives us information about the number of brainwave cycles/rhythmic pulses we produce per second (on the Hertz scale):

- The beta state is the normal, outwardly focused state of an adult, with brainwaves oscillating roughly between 13 and 38 cycles per second.
- We exhibit brainwaves in the alpha frequency, about 8–12 cycles per second, when we relax, meditate, daydream, focus intently on a creative activity or perform a ceremony. This state is also known as the 'here and now' state.
- Theta waves, 4–7 cycles per second, become dominant in 'twilight' states, such as the ones we experience just before falling asleep, in very deep meditation or when we are lucid dreaming (when we are dreaming and know we are dreaming). They have also been measured during intense contemporary shamanic journeys.
- Delta waves, fewer than 4 cycles per second, are generated when we sleep. They have also been measured in 'death and rebirth' rituals in shamanism.

Recently, via functioning magnetic resonance imaging (fMRI) brain scans, we have also been able to observe which brain regions are active and which are less active when we alter our state. Research demonstrates that people who have been involved in meditation and similar spiritual practices over long periods of time, or have had extreme experiences such as NDEs, display positive changes in the brain that seem to be permanent.[1]

We also know that when we focus inwardly, we automatically increase the electronic activity in certain parts of our brain (e.g. memory parts and visual parts) whilst calming down the activity in other parts (e.g. parts that process information from our environment or 'logical thinking parts').

What we access when we alter our state

Altering our state enables us to access wide-ranging information, with fluid boundaries, depending on many factors.[2] What we access depends on what we intend to access and how profoundly we alter our perception. It includes:

Material from our personal subconscious

Psychology has shown beyond doubt that when we alter our state we can access personal material that usually lies hidden on different levels of the personal subconscious/unconscious realm, which stores vast amounts of information. This material can take various forms: memories and past experiences, images, associations to a theme, deeply held beliefs, strong emotions and so on.

We can say that such personal material is accessed in the alpha state.

Transpersonal realms

On the next level, beyond the personal, we enter transpersonal realms that are more difficult to describe. A shaman would call them the 'spirit worlds', some people call them 'the level of soul' and in our society they are known as the realms of the 'collective unconscious', as defined by

C.G. Jung.[3] The consensus view is that these realms hold material that we don't acquire individually, as it is either genetically transmitted or held in a 'pool of consciousness or other dimensions', but can nevertheless access when we alter our state of perception. The content of these realms is universal, likely to be recognized anywhere in the world and presents itself in our brain in archetypal form.

Archetypes are more than images. They are 'knowing patterns' that are built into our psyche, associated with meaning and translated into images. They are drawn from myth, fairy tales, folklore and spiritual and psychological teachings. They can take the form of humanoids, such as the Mother, the Hero, the Goddess and the Teacher, or animals and mystical creatures, such as the Serpent, the Jaguar, the Eagle, the Unicorn and the Dragon. They can also be more like concepts, such as the Self, the Shadow, the Anima/Animus and figures of Death and Rebirth.

In shamanism, the transpersonal realm with all its archetypal elements has been thoroughly explored and in some traditions precisely categorized. The figures, materials and events are seen as arising from levels of the multi-dimensional reality to which a person's consciousness, energy body or soul can travel. The traditional shaman would refer to some of the figures as 'spirits'. For example, if you were to dream about your grandmother, the shaman would see her, if she presented herself in a certain way, as an ancestral spirit connecting with them in the 'dreamworld', an energetic realm as real as any other.[4]

In some contemporary schools it is postulated that we need to be in the theta state to access the transpersonal realms.

Extreme visionary states: beyond the limits of the ordinary

Whilst we can all learn to alter our state enough to access archetypal material, extreme altered states take this further, opening gateways to dimensions beyond those we are normally able to experience. The closest we can come to describing these states is to call them 'out-of-body experiences', 'near-death and rebirth experiences', 'dis-memberment visions' and 'profound lucid dreams'. Some can be induced by taking psychedelic plant medicines. The brain is mostly in delta state whilst these experiences take place.

Such extreme altered states, and the realms entered during them, are part of the training and initiation of traditional shamans worldwide. They are not the norm in contemporary shamanism, but can be sought when we get deeply involved in shamanic practice. (I have been through a dismemberment experience and attended initiation rituals that were designed to induce extreme states and near-death experiences.) This book will not provide exercises that lead you into extreme states, but I will describe them briefly, as some knowledge is necessary to understand the shamanic view of the world.

Everybody who has experienced or studied such states, myself included, acknowledges that they are transformative. They dismantle our identity and change our sense of who we are and what the world is about.

The literature about the training and initiation processes of traditional shamans shows that the shaman has to go through such transformational processes to expand consciousness, to become skilled in traversing and working in all the realms we can access and to synthesize the fragmented parts of the psyche into a harmonious whole.

A well-known example of such a transformational process is the initiation of the Lakota shaman Black Elk. He became very ill at the age of nine and spent 12 days unconscious and on the brink of death. In one of his visions during that period, he saw the six grandfathers, representing the west, south, north and east, the sky and the Earth. Each of them gave him certain powers and he was shown how the world worked. According to members of his tribe, he emerged a changed person. He describes his 'strangeness' afterwards and his inability to put into words all the images, feelings and words he had been presented with:

> *And while I stood there I saw more than I can tell and understood more than I saw; for I was seeing in a sacred manner the shapes of all things in the spirit, and the shape of all shapes as they must live together like one being. And I saw that the sacred hoop of my people was one of many hoops that made one circle, wide as daylight and as starlight, and in the centre grew one mighty flowering tree to shelter all the children of one mother and one father. And I saw that it was holy.*[5]

Another description of the visionary world accessed in extreme states comes from my friend Matthew Pallamary, a shamanic writer who works with sacred medicine plants in the Amazon. It gives an idea of the energy fields that can be accessed:

> *[These visions] speak through colours, patterns, abstractions, and archetypes, introducing concepts*

> *beyond limited rational thinking. Moreover, the language of teacher plants unfolds their cosmic wisdom, blossoming in geometric permutations that speak in mathematical progressions using the universal language of sacred geometry to reveal the true nature of the divine unfolding of conscious intelligence that permeates all that is.*[6]

Another form of extreme state experiences are dismemberment visions, during which the shaman's body is taken apart and reassembled in a different way, which transforms them and gives them power. These rather frightening death and rebirth experiences have been reported globally. The spirits shamans encounter during dismemberment give them power, but also have to be wrestled with and learned from. The laws of the other realms have to be mastered, too.

> *The initiatory visions of a Yakut Shaman includes dying in a three-day ritual, being dismembered and then put back together. The Mongolian shamans' initiations – in the Tungus, Buryat, Manchu and Ostyak tribes – include ritual dismemberment, death and resurrection, involving shamanic ancestors. Australian shamans have their bellies opened by a supernatural being called the Nagatya who places crystals within the body, which give them magical powers. Some Eskimo shamans report being devoured by animals so that new 'shaman flesh' can grow and in many African tribes the shaman's head is removed and the brain is restored to give the shaman spirit vision.*[7]

These transformational experiences take place whilst the body is 'dead or nearly dead' and the consciousness or energy body is in the other realms.

That the consciousness can indeed travel whilst the body is clinically dead has been confirmed by contemporary research. A profound study by the Dutch cardiologist Pim van Lommel has shown that most patients who report near-death experiences travel outside the body to realms beyond normally perceived reality.[8] Although the NDEs studied in contemporary literature are a far cry from the experiences traditional shamans go through during their death and rebirth periods, the research confirms that NDEs are transformational: they change patients' self-concept and what they believe their consciousness to be, as well as their world-view and attitudes towards life and death. Van Lommel found that after an NDE, patients lost their fear of death, showed heightened intuitiveness and believed that the soul lived on in other dimensions. They did not acquire the power of the traditional shaman, but love and compassion for self, others and nature became dominant values and material strivings became insignificant. Like others before him, van Lommel came to the conclusion that there was a strong case for the existence of 'other dimensions' in which our consciousness or soul lives on after death and which can be accessed via extreme altered states before physical death – something which is quite normal in traditional shamanism.

The shamanic view of the world

The traditional shamanic world-view, which is shared by contemporary shamanism (although sometimes described in more modern terms), is based on the profound experiences shamans have within altered states and other realms. It is also informed by their intense connections with the natural world, their rites and initiations, and the knowledge passed on to them by their ancestors, teachers and spirit teachers. Here are the key concepts:

Everything is made of vibrations/energy fields and is connected

Experiencing and exploring reality from different planes of consciousness, shamans perceive the universe in the form of vibrations and energy fields and come to the only possible conclusion: the universe is a living being, energetic/vibrational in essence, in which everything is connected. Or, in other words, the world beyond the materially visible one is an evolving web of vibrating fields, which we would now call the 'quantum realm' or 'the pool of consciousness'.

It is worth mentioning here that this view seems to be increasingly confirmed by science, especially by physics, higher mathematics and biology, and is now being used as the basis of ecology and energy psychology.[9]

Everything contains a life-force essence: spirit

Connected to the view that, on a deeper level, everything vibrates and is energetically interdependent is the notion that everything contains an energetic essence. In shamanism this is called 'spirit'.

'Everything' means literally *everything*: animals, rocks, plants, rivers, lakes, oceans, stars, galaxies, humans. 'Spirit', in contemporary terms, consists of vibrating patterns that carry information. So if we refer to the spirit of a particular plant, star, person, animal, stone or any object we can think of, we are talking about its unique vibrating patterns and, most importantly, the information these patterns carry.

It is this spirit essence, loaded with information, that makes a being what it is – a human a human and a tree a tree – but it also transcends this because it is a basic life-force that exists throughout the universe, manifesting in different forms.[10]

There is a source: Spirit, Great Mystery or Great Spirit

The vibrating life-force essence called spirit is not to be confused with the terms 'Great Spirit' or 'Spirit' or 'Great Mystery', which are used to describe a creation source from which the life-force essence stems. As the name 'Great Mystery' implies, we don't know its precise nature. We only know that it is seen as an original source that manifests in countless forms within a universe that creates and recreates itself and has no limits in time and space. This source is undivided and whole, and is perceived as being sacred in every traditional shamanic culture.

To understand this concept better, we could replace 'Spirit' or 'Great Mystery' with the more contemporary terms 'Source' or 'Oneness'. So there is this Source, this Oneness, which is perceived in all spiritual systems as being undivided and from which all aspects of creation arise. This source can only create if it divides, or, as Deepak Chopra says: 'Out of itself, Oneness creates the many.'[11] If we look at nature, we can see that all life evolved from a single cell-division or, if we look at the Big Bang theory, there was an explosion of something whole that then divided. In spiritual terms, we talk about creation from the original Source.

Everything is sacred and evolving

Now, if this is so, then all the different aspects of creation, past and future, are already, in the form of potentialities, inherent in this original Source. If we take this further and postulate, as many have done lately, that the still-expanding universe has a holographic quality, based on the physicist David Bohm's theories, then all the potentialities, as well as the original Oneness, are everywhere, because from the first moment of division onwards, the 'potentiality within the original source' is reflected holographically throughout the universe.[12] This is, as far as I understand it, what the 15th-century Indian mystic poet Kabir means when he says, 'Wherever you are is the entry point,' and what Black Elk means when he says, 'Everywhere is the centre of the world. Everything is sacred.'

Following on from this is the shamanic notion that everything is evolving in a 'sacred dance of creation'. It is in a state of 'becoming'. If we look at expressions such as 'All life is sacred' or 'Nothing should be done to harm the children', we understand that shamanism entails striving for a life that honours the sacredness and continuity of creation.

We are spirit in essence

In the shamanic world-view, we, like everything else, are essentially spirit in manifested form, albeit a rather complex one. Therefore our lives are expressions of a spiritual intention, a potentiality seeking to manifest itself at its fullest: we, too, are in a state of 'becoming'.

I personally have struggled with this concept of 'becoming' and have concluded that it ultimately means developing to our highest level of possibility and ultimately to our highest possible level of consciousness, individually as well as collectively (human consciousness development is far from over).

We have a soul

So, we are spirit, which is the underlying life-force. But in both traditional and contemporary shamanism you might encounter a differentiation between 'spirit' and 'soul'. Some cultures assume one soul, whilst others speak of three souls. Here it suffices to make a general distinction between soul and spirit.

Spirit, as an essence, contains all the life-force possibilities there are – in potential form all that we as humans can become. The part of us that knows this and drives us to become all we can be is our individual soul. Our soul also knows the energetic imprints we carry in the form of individual and collective experiences (which some call karma). So it is our soul that provides us with an inner voice, compass and direction, reminding us, often in little whispers, that there is more, and it is our soul that suffers if we don't follow this 'spiritual path of becoming'.

Our soul can be altered by our experiences during every lifetime. It can be split, diminished and hurt. In shamanism, it is assumed that it is mainly the 'loss of soul' that causes emotional, physical and mental disease as well as a diminishing of vital life energy. An important task of the shaman is to travel to different worlds to bring back these soul parts and reintegrate them in the individual or the community.

Spirits are energetic entities

Spirits, from a shamanic point of view, are entities in these different worlds – the spirit realms. They are experienced as non-material and intelligent, and they provide the shaman with information, power, energy, help and wisdom.[13]

The shaman always works with spirits, especially with guides and spirit helpers, ancestral spirits, animal spirits and nature spirits, and cultivates a profound and respectful relationships with them.

Everything is treated as being real

Shamans are on the whole not too concerned with what can be proven, at least not in a scientific sense. From a shamanic perspective, everything that can be experienced is real, whether it exists in the form of matter or the form of energy and whether we experience it in our normal state of mind or in an altered state.

So, in shamanism, parallel universes, different layers of reality, infinite possibilities, immanent potentialities and various states of consciousness are not puzzling. For the shaman, there is no sense of the 'natural' versus the 'supernatural', or 'reality' versus 'fantasy'. There is only that which we can see and that which is hidden, and the visible and invisible are not only connected but equally real.

Chapter 4
Shamanic Territories

In shamanism we use various maps and models to depict the planes of reality and consciousness. They give us a sense of the territory and tools to work with, but they cannot depict the whole of reality, so leave room for different interpretations and adaptations. I will introduce you to three maps: the *axis mundi*, the cosmic spirit worlds and the four levels of human perception. All are widely used and have been adapted by contemporary practitioners.

The *axis mundi*

The *axis mundi*, also known as the cosmic axis, the cosmic tree and the centre of the world, is seen as a central axis that runs from the Earth to the sky, connecting the worlds. We find it in one form or another in almost all religions, philosophies and ancient cultures. It can take the form of places, such as mountains and hills, or images, such as trees, vines, pillars and staffs, and sometimes we find man-made structures, such as temples and pyramids, built in places that are seen as centres of the world.[1]

In shamanism, the *axis mundi* often takes the form of a tree. This cosmic tree has taken on many variations over time and place. The Iroquois' cosmic tree stands at the centre of the world with its branches supporting the sun and the moon whilst its roots penetrate the primal Great Turtle, which carries the Earth on its back. There is a Mayan myth of the 'First Tree', based on the ancient concept of the tree of life, which has also been used, for instance, in Genesis as the tree of knowledge. We find a tree with five branches in India and Persia. Siberian and Mongolian shamans utilize the world tree to ascend to the upper world for initiation ceremonies. It is also the home of ancestral souls. Our Christmas tree derives from the pagan cosmic tree in Scandinavia, and Buddha became enlightened under the Bodhi tree in Bodh Gaya, India.

The central idea around the cosmic tree – often depicted with a solid trunk, wide-spread branches that reach into the sky and roots that reach deep into the Earth – has remained the same over time and in various cultures. It connects the three worlds or cosmic zones: the upper, middle and lower worlds, or the sky, Earth and underworlds. These three worlds are also the planes of consciousness accessible via altered states. In shamanism we can pass through an opening in the cosmic tree and travel to all worlds and all times.

The three cosmic worlds

The three basic cosmic levels – the upper, lower and middle worlds, connected via the cosmic tree – are non-linear, timeless and infinite. They exist independently of the human mind but also form the different planes of human consciousness. Together they make up 'the whole'.

The lower and upper worlds are energetic realities, sometimes called non-ordinary realities, which we are rarely aware of in normal waking consciousness but which can be accessed in altered states. The middle world is twofold: it consists of both the invisible energetic aspects of the everyday world we live in and the visible material aspects of it.[2]

The lower world

The lower world, or underworld, is mostly pictured as a landscape, with mountains, deserts, forests, rivers, oceans, caves, valleys, jungles or combinations of these. It is the home of the spirits of animals, trees, plants and rocks, as well as human-like spirits that are connected to the mystery of the Earth.

The lower world is also the world where we find 'the shadows'. The stories of the underworld are myths and fairy tales, mostly involving an encounter with a dark force. Frightening, devious, evil or monstrous beings can populate the lower world of the shaman's clients, be they individuals or the community. The lower world is also concerned with the human psyche: our cut-off shadow aspects can be found there and our split-off soul parts will mostly flee there.

Shamans work regularly in the lower world and have extensive knowledge of it. They, and indigenous people in general, own the whole – the dark and the light – and they have devised many ways and means, such as rituals, prayers, journeys and soul retrieval, to work with them and transform and integrate them.

The lower world is accessed via a journey through an imagined opening or portal into the Earth in the form of the roots of the cosmic tree, a tunnel, a hole in the ground, a well or anything that leads down. The knowing that we receive when we access the lower worlds, for instance via a shamanic journey or ceremonial means, is more instinctual than intellectual, providing us with images, sudden insights, emotional reactions, energetic forces and – quite an important aspect in all the worlds – it will be shown and taught to us by our spirit helpers. The spirit helpers of the lower world appear mainly in the form of power animals (*see page 66*).

The upper world

The upper world(s) appear and feel quite different from the lower world. They often appear as etheric realms of many layers. The light is brighter here, colours are usually more pastel and somehow fuzzy, and the whole place feels quite airy. Crystal structures, cloudlike realms and cosmic beings can be encountered.

The upper world is traditionally accessed via the branches of the cosmic tree, ropes, staircases leading upwards, high mountains, rainbows or smoke. It is inhabited by helping spirits, powerful teachers in humanoid form, formless spirit beings and ancestral spirits. Sandra Ingerman remarks that the upper worlds are 'formed by the dreaming of the higher gods and goddesses, the ancestors, the ascended masters, the compassionate angelic forces that are willing to be of service to us – most often as teachers and guides'.[3]

In the upper world we seek guidance and wisdom, and what we perceive and receive is not instinctual, but rather has philosophical and wise qualities in the sense that it is knowledge that seems to reach beyond 'what we know'.

In the upper world we can connect with our spirit guides and teachers and our ancestors in spirit form. Some contemporary shamanic teachers also recommend we look for our own 'higher self' within those realms. This is our transpersonal aspect, sometimes also called the over-soul, the immortal aspect of ourselves that can communicate with us through dreams and visions and be a source of intuition, inspiration and guidance.

The middle world

The twofold middle world consists of our everyday physical reality and the underlying energetic reality - the 'spirit aspect' - of the physical universe we live in. This is where the mental, emotional, physical and spiritual energy fields of living humanity and the spirits of manifest nature flow in patterns. It is where psychic phenomena happen, thought forms exist, synchronicities are observed, hunches and omens are received and telepathy is believed to be possible. Healing work may take place in these energy fields and cures be sought either before or after someone becomes physically ill.

Middle-world journeys are mainly used to communicate with the nature spirits that exist within our realm, such as the spirits of trees, plants, rocks, the sun and moon and, in some cultures, nature spirit people.

To access the middle world, the shaman enters an altered state and floats through the realm, merging and communicating with those energies. In a healing ritual, for instance, they might travel to the middle world to gather facts about people, animals and plants that are significant to the illness of the person in need and then perform extractions and cleansings of the energy fields and provide the herbal and other medicines needed.

In some teachings, it is stated that some middle-world work can be difficult because the energy fields and spirits there can be negative, detrimental or outright evil. This can be the case in war zones or places that have witnessed much suffering and cruelty. Also, souls who haven't made their way over to the higher planes, perhaps as the result of a traumatic death, are trapped in the middle world.

The four levels of human perception

Another map I will use in this book consists of four hierarchically ordered levels of human perception:

- the physical
- the emotional/mental
- the soul
- the spirit

This ties in with the distinction between 'soul' and 'spirit' described earlier. There are slightly different animal representations of these levels in various cultures, but as the animals represent the energies of the levels, their appearance is of minor importance.

- *The physical* level is represented by the *Serpent*. It is our body, our instinctual knowing and our senses. This level guides us when the sensual and instinctual are required. It knows nature, danger and opportunity. It is also the level where we act physically in a physical world. It is the level of beta brainwaves, where our brain is active in an outwardly focused way in the waking state.

- *The mental/emotional* level is represented by the *Jaguar*. It is the level where we feel and think. The Jaguar is a great hunter, stalking its prey, planning its route and changing quickly when required to ensure a successful hunt. It represents our mental capacity, enabling us to plan, think, be emotionally involved and bring our visions and dreams to fruition in the material world. When we relax, go into a meditative state and focus inwardly, we enter the alpha state and can bring this level to our awareness.
- *The soul* level is represented by the *Hummingbird*, which is aware of our soul's journey. This is the level we are on when we are on a profound shamanic journey or very deeply immersed in ceremonial work. Here we can create, have visions and encounter spirits. On this level our intent has great power and we are the energetic co-creators we are meant to be. We can experience this level when we are in theta – when we are in a deep trance state.
- *The spirit level* is represented by the *Eagle*. It is the domain of spirit, the realm where everything already exists in potential form. This is knowing on the highest level and in shamanic terms we do not need to change anything here, because the bigger picture is shown to us and all is well. We are at the level of 'Oneness', of just Being. Some call it the level of enlightenment. Our

> brain sinks down into delta waves or even lower, to a state where we hardly exist but are one with the whole.

In shamanism we are asked to become aware at which level we are functioning. We strive to use our senses and instincts on the physical level, be aware of our mental and emotional capacities and states and use them wisely on that level, to dream and create on the level of soul and, on the spirit level, to become aware of our soul's path and strive to expand our consciousness to reach the highest level of knowing.

Part II

AWAKENING THE SHAMANIC FORCE WITHIN

'The shaman is a self-realized person. She discovers the ways of Spirit through her inner awakening.'

ALBERTO VILLOLDO, *SHAMAN, HEALER, SAGE*

Chapter 5

Bringing the Shamanic Dimension into Your Daily Life

Shamanism will enchant you, especially once you begin to appreciate the many means, approaches, tools and pathways it offers. This chapter lays the foundations that will enable you to begin to bring a shamanic dimension into your daily life. After introducing you to a few essential skills, you will learn how to create an altar and work with sacred space, how to call spirit and work with it, how to develop your own daily ritual and how to create and utilize power objects.

As you continue reading this book and your shamanic practice intensifies and deepens, you will be able to develop these skills and tools and use them whenever required, no matter which path you choose. We now have the freedom to choose the pathways that work for us. For some people, medicine dancing, drumming and vibrational sound work become the major pathways, whilst others are more inclined to learn from, and in, nature, and love vision quests, nature spirit communication and nature camps. Some take to shamanic journeying like ducks to water, whilst lucid dreaming, storytelling or medicine plant teachings offer the right pathways for others. Many seekers use combinations of these means, though some are more inclined to follow one traditional teaching path. Whatever feels right to you, if you explore it and follow it, your shamanic path will unfold.

Basic skills and tools

No matter what you attempt with shamanic means, you need to be able to tune into – and work with – the underlying energetic realities. Often you need to be tuned into both realities at once: the material one and the underlying energetic one. Developing an understanding of various tools and skills and practising using them will enhance your knowledge about the underlying forces that shape your life and help you to influence them. It will keep you tuned into the levels that really matter: soul and spirit. As Jung said, 'Only if we know the thing which truly matters is the infinite can we avoid fixing our interests upon futilities and upon all kinds of goals which are not of real importance.'[1]

The importance and power of your intent

For the shaman, everything begins with an intent, held with focus and clarity. Intent is a kind of vision, a goal, an outcome you want to achieve. It has to be formulated clearly and held attentively. It is more than a statement in the form of a sentence, such as 'I am going to journey to the upper world' or 'I am creating this ceremony for healing.' As your intent directs the energies of what you are attempting to do, as well as manifests the energies of the outcome, it needs to be absorbed into your being and into your task. Therefore you need to hold it in your heart and mind and focus on it.

The real power of your intent lies in the fact that it bridges the ordinary and non-ordinary realities. It influences the energetic worlds and therefore also this reality. In other words, your intent is, at its most powerful, the overlap point of the goal you have in mind and its manifestation.

For example, when you create a ceremony to let something go and call something in, your intent might be formulated along the lines of: 'I am creating this ceremony to let go of my fear and to call in courage.' This intent will first infuse much of what you include in the ceremony, from how you set it up to the offering you create, from the ritual you use to the spirits you call in. Then, as you hold the intent – letting go of your fear and bringing courage into your life – with focus throughout the ceremony, it directs the energies during the ceremony, and the more impeccably you stay with this, the more likely it is that your intent will manifest.

Receptivity and deep listening: hearing the voice of spirit

All spiritual practice requires us to be receptive, to be silent and listen deeply with all our senses. To be receptive is a passive skill, a quality of the feminine which, in a world orientated towards the masculine principle of 'doing and expressing', is greatly undervalued. No matter if you are on a shamanic journey, connecting to nature, asking for help from spirit, conducting a ceremony or just wanting to know what you are feeling or intuiting or what spirit is telling you, you have to be receptive. This means being still enough to hear, see and feel what is happening on deeper levels of reality.

As long as our mind is chattering away or we are busy 'doing', it's difficult to hear the voice of our soul or experience a sudden intuitive knowing or become aware of messages. So, if you don't already meditate, I would advise you to attempt it as a practice. Besides being beneficial for your mental and physical wellbeing, just sitting and being still every day will help you to develop the skill to tune into the level of soul and receive its messages. It is essential to understand that you cannot hear the voice of spirit if you do not listen.

Altering your state and working with spirit

All shamanic work takes place in altered states and with spirit. This means that most of the time you will use some means to go into a (light) trance state, to still yourself, to focus and absorb yourself completely in the task, shutting out the clutter of the world around you and the chatter of your mind. Some practices, such as trance dancing, lead you quickly and naturally into an altered state. Others are directly designed to help you alter your state or perception. For instance, when you begin to journey (*see Chapter 6*), it is best to download the drumming recording that I have provided for you (*see* www.christamackinnon.com). It works because the beat of the drum is adjusted to the theta wavelength of the brain. For other practices, such as ceremonial work, medicine wheel journeys or work in nature, follow the instructions given in this book, which will tune you into deeper levels.

All shamanic work also requires the presence of spirit, which is called in at the beginning of shamanic endeavours, as I will show you below. With focus, it will tune you into deeper levels, open sacred space and bring in the energies required.

Developing trust when working with energies

As you begin shamanic practices you will have to develop a sense for energies and trust in whatever you experience, feel or sense and how it translates into images, words or intuitive knowing. For instance, when you begin to access the spirit worlds, you will experience whatever happens on an energetic level as images, emotions, sudden insights or thoughts, but sometimes also just as a kind of knowing or as energy forms such as swirling or geometrical patterns, colours or strong forces. Keep in mind that you are working with energies and that the way they present themselves to you is right for you.

There is a big debate as to whether the spirit worlds are 'real', in the sense that they exist as energetic worlds parallel to our manifest world, or are 'just in our imagination', or are part of a level of consciousness that has been created by humankind, such as the collective unconscious. In practical terms, it really doesn't matter which of those cosmologies you subscribe to, because as long as you work with clear intent, focus and the help of spirit, you can trust that whatever shows itself or happens to you is right.

Vibrational tools in shamanism

Vibrations are very important in shamanism and therefore drums, rattles and sound are used to create various levels of vibration for various purposes, such as to seal sacred space, to call in spirit forces, or for healing, journeying, trance dancing, ceremony and more.

I will come back to tools and how to use them in later chapters, but when you get deeper into shamanic practice it is a good idea to acquire either a rattle or a drum. Most people start with a rattle, because they are cheaper to buy and easier to use. Find one that really speaks to you and charge it with power (*see page 58*).

Working with spirit: calling the spirit forces

Although they know their craft and have refined their skills, shamans state that it is spirit that works with and through them. Therefore, no matter what you are doing – journeying, creating a ceremony, healing, trance dancing, dreaming, questing for vision or connecting with nature – it is important to ask spirit to be with you.

In the following chapters I will give you some guidance on how to call in spirit for specific tasks. But generally speaking, in shamanism we call:

- the spirits of the four directions
- all there is above and all there is below and Great Spirit/ Great Mystery
- ancestral spirits, if appropriate
- the spirits of our 'relations' (such as nature or animal spirits), if appropriate
- the spirit allies and helpers that can support us in our specific task

Exercise: Calling spirit

Here's a basic example. You can use it for almost everything and adapt it as required:

> *East: 'I call the powers of the east, the spirit of the sun, of light, illumination, creativity.'*
>
> *South: 'I call the powers of the south, the spirit of water, of the plant kingdom, of trust and flowing.'*
>
> *West: 'I call the powers of the west, the spirit of Mother Earth, of introspection, of the dreamlodge [the place of looking within].'*[2]
>
> *North: 'I call the powers of the north, the spirit of air, of the animal kingdom, of wisdom, clarity and discernment.'*
>
> *Above and Below: 'I call all there is above and all there is below and Great Spirit to be with me/us during [e.g. this ceremony] so that all I/we do is not only for my/our own good, but for the greater good of all.'*

Calling spirit with heartfelt sincerity and focus, saying the calls aloud, is more important than trying to adhere to a set ritual or formula. When I call, I beat my drum softly and I also turn in the direction to which I'm calling.

As I said earlier, you can adjust this basic calling to your intent. If you were working with the feminine, for instance, you would also call in the Goddess or the feminine powers. You can also call in helpful ancestral spirits or, as most people do, include your specific spirit allies (*see Chapter 6*).

A sense of the sacred: create an altar and clear your space

As already stated, shamanic work involves working with energies, particularly to develop a sense of the sacred and to strive to bring it actively into your life. As spirit underlies everything, you will find that the sacred is everywhere and that you can enhance it and bring it to the fore in your daily life. A good way to begin is to create an altar, a space which is sacred for you and which you can dedicate to your connection with spirit.

Another step, which for most people follows instinctively, is to develop a feeling for the space around you, to cleanse your space on a regular basis, to declutter it, to pay attention to the objects with which you surround yourself and to infuse it all with good intent – with the sacred.

Creating an altar

An altar is a physical home for spirit and a threshold between the worlds. It can be indoors or outdoors, permanent or portable. Your personal altar holds your spiritual intent and is a focal point for the sacred in your life. It assists you in your spiritual undertakings, be they meditation, rituals, ceremonies, quests or healing.

The objects on an altar are more than symbolic representations: they hold the very energy and power of that which they represent. For instance, when the shaman invites certain spirits to attend a ceremony, it is believed that their energies reside in the objects on the altar for the course of the ceremony.

An altar is not static, although a basic structure such as a wheel is often used and the main objects often stay the same. But generally speaking, a shamanic altar is alive. It will be adjusted according to the work you are doing and your own development, and it will, over time, take on a life of its own. You may, for example, want to represent your spirit helpers (*see Chapter 6*) or to craft an object with the intent of bringing something into your life (*see below*).

Lately I have become interested in the feminine, and a friend gave me a beautiful necklace signifying this. That necklace lies now on my altar. When I facilitate groups for women, I take it off the altar and wear it. I also have a black stone on my altar, which I hold in my hand when I do soul retrieval. It has been with me for about 15 years and was first energized by one of my teachers, a Brazilian shaman. I treat this stone with care and respect. I clean it and place it back on the altar when the soul-retrieval session is finished, so it can rest and re-energize.

Your altar should be personal and meaningful to you. Below are guidelines for a basic design:

- *A cloth:* use a piece of fabric that is beautiful and meaningful to you. I currently use a bright yellow cloth that I brought back from Mongolia.
- *A centrepiece:* most people use a candle, signifying 'that which always was and will always be'. I use a candle within a small circle of stone people.
- *The four directions of the wheel:* leaving a bit of distance around the centrepiece, build up the four directions. I use crystals and stones, one in each direction: in the

east a red calcite, the south a blue crystal, the west an obsidian and the north a clear quartz. I chose these for their colours and because each holds a story significant to me.

- *The four elements:* I also include the four elements of earth, air, fire and water in my basic structure. Flowers or small branches represent earth. A beautiful feather represents air. A tea light in front of a small Buddha statue given to me by my daughter represents fire and a small shell represents water.
- *Other power objects:* besides a basic altar, you can add power objects (*see below*), as long as they have meaning for you and are put there with a spiritual intent.

My altar is, in my eyes, sacred, harmonious and beautiful, because spirit and I like beauty. Some altars I have come across are very powerful, but not what I would call 'beautiful', and others are very beautiful, but feel like a piece of art rather than 'sacred'. As long as your altar engages the sacred, it is best that you find your own way.

Exercise: How to create your basic altar

Take some time to construct your altar. Be aware that you can change it, but don't wait for 'all the right objects' to show up before you start. If you can find a cloth you like, a candle for the centre and four stones to mark the four directions, you can get started. From there your altar will grow naturally.

- Collect and cleanse the objects you want to put on the altar. Either wash them and leave them in the air to dry or smudge them (*see below*).

- Sit for a while to still yourself. Call in spirit. State your intent – namely, creating an altar – and invite spirit to infuse your altar with beneficial energy.
- Next, take each object into your hands before putting it on the altar and ask spirit to 'accept this as [whatever it represents]'. Hold it for a while and energize it with your intent. Energizing the object is important because your objects will, over time, turn into power objects, which I will describe later in this chapter (see *page 58*). Say the intent aloud when you place the object on the altar. For example, when you place the object that represents the east and fire on the altar you could say, 'This stone represents the east. It represents the illumination, spirit and creativity in my life' or 'I ask spirit to bring illumination and creativity into my life.' Do this with each object.
- Afterwards, drum or rattle around the altar space (or use whatever else feels right) to seal the energy into the space and then sit for a while meditating on your creation. You might find that you already get some ideas about putting more on the altar, or taking something away, or that an item on the altar begins to 'speak to you'. Be creative.
- Finally, thank spirit for their help and ask for their blessing on your altar.

Remember that the items on your altar are there to be containers of spirit. They hold the energy of what they represent and are there to be used and worked with. As Don Martin Pinedo, a shaman from Peru, says: 'The mesa is an altar that gives vision, power, and spiritual connection to everything ... You must use and value your mesa or you will lose your power and your connections.'[3]

Clearing and infusing space with beauty and the sacred

Space, like everything else, has power. It either supports you or it doesn't. Paying attention to the energies in the space that surrounds you is really beneficial to your wellbeing and your spiritual connection.

In shamanism, clearing/cleansing a space or a person's energy body is usually done with smoke. The easiest way to do this is to use either sage or sweet grass. You light it in a bowl, blow out the flame and use a feather to distribute the smoke. If you don't like the smell of sage or sweet grass, use incense or, if you dislike smoke altogether, use a sage spray.

Exercise: Cleansing your space

- Stand for a moment and sense what the space needs. Does it feel heavy, or too airy and ungrounded? Has it been contaminated by arguments or too much rushing around? Does it feel stale or unsettling? Trust whatever you sense or feel.
- Next, call in spirit. You can keep this really simple:

  'I call spirit to help me to clear the space.'

- Then state your intent aloud:

  'I am cleansing this space. I ask spirit to help me to infuse it with the energy beneficial to me and everybody who enters this house/space/room.'

- Then just walk around and smudge/spray the space. Pay attention to what you sense. Some corners need more than others; some rooms need a second round of cleansing. State your intent as often as it feels right, hold it in your mind as well as your heart and ask for spirit's help as often as feels necessary.

Decluttering your space is also important in the long term. We live in a cluttered world full of unnecessary objects and also of information, consumption and entertainment. You can influence how clear and focused you are and how uncluttered you feel by clearing your space. William Morris' statement offers a good guideline, now more than ever: 'Have nothing in your houses that you do not know to be useful, or believe to be beautiful.' Everything else takes you away from what is important: that which lies beneath.

Find a daily ritual to connect with spirit

Now that you have an altar and know how to call in spirit, you might want to create a small daily ritual for yourself. This is a wonderful way of starting and ending the day, as it will connect you to the sacred, to spirit and to yourself.

A morning ritual

Most people who work in a shamanic way will do a small ceremony, maybe tuning into and greeting the directions in the morning, asking for guidance and setting an intent for the day and including a blessing for the Earth. I like to keep my morning ritual brief, based on the knowledge that if it is too elaborate I might not do it when pressed for time. I have a basic ritual which I adjust for different contexts and needs. I love my morning ritual and usually perform it outside.

For my morning ritual, I go outside, close my eyes, tune into my heart space, breathe into it and then tune into my surroundings.

Then I step into the middle of an imagined wheel and greet the Earth, calling in the spirits of the four directions and all there is above and below.

Next, I turn to each of the four directions, tuning into the element of each. Speaking aloud, I greet each direction and bestow a blessing.

Afterwards, I again tune into myself and my surroundings, take a few breaths and still myself, and then, from the centre, standing still but moving my arms in all-encompassing circles, I bless 'all the environment', 'all the people I love' and 'all my relations' (meaning all living beings) and 'my work'. I often also ask spirit to bless my work and to be with me during my day and thank it for all the gifts and blessings bestowed upon me.

This takes me around 10 minutes, depending on how long and deeply I tune into things. Sometimes, I receive simple insights or messages during the ritual, but my intent is generally to tune in, to greet, to bless and to give thanks.

There are many ways to design your ritual. Some people light a candle, sit for a while, tune into themselves and the environment and then imagine that they are bestowing blessings as the light of the candle is sent out into the world. If you want to work with your altar, you can use the stones or crystals on it, holding each in turn and working through and with them. Some people like to dance their ritual, using music and movement and dancing their intent.

Whatever the ritual you design, be creative and involve your body as much as you can. Step literally into the centre, turn literally to the directions, move your hands and arms in gestures and say your intents, blessings and thanks out loud. A ritual is meditative, but not a meditation in the classical sense.

An evening ritual

An evening ritual involves giving thanks and letting go. I perform a small one most evenings, during which I give thanks for the day and let go of things that I do not want to carry forwards into the night. In contrast to my morning ritual, I often perform the evening one inside.

You can design an evening ritual in a similar way to your morning ritual. If you have had a very hectic day or feel quite detached from yourself, having been involved in lots of things that have led you outside yourself and outside the sacred, you might want to spend a bit more time stilling yourself or dancing yourself back into your body, utilizing music or drumming.

> *For my evening ritual, I do something similar to my morning ritual, but instead of bestowing greetings and blessings, I give thanks to the spirits of the directions and to all there is above and below. If I need to let things go, I imagine that I am letting them float away from me into the Earth or up into the sky and asking for the issue to be transmuted into something positive.*

Again, I involve my body as much as feels right and I speak out loud.

Embodying energy in matter: power objects

In shamanism we frequently work with power objects. These objects embody and hold particular energies/vibrations, which are utilized for specific tasks, such as ceremonial work, healing, integration, energy transfer, manifestation or grounding.

The general concept of embodiment is based on the interchange between the physical and the energetic, meaning that we can enclose – and of course also express – an energy force or essence within and through a material body. This body – in the form of our own physical body, an object or a place – functions as a container for specific vibrations. Objects that are used for healing hold healing energy, whilst ceremonial objects hold the energy of the ceremonial intent and the spirits at work in the ceremony. Drums, rattles and other instruments also hold energy: the energy of the animal that gave its hide for the drum, the energy and intent of the drum-maker, the energies of the intents and prayers of the drummer and so on. Places, such as altars, burial grounds or sacred sites, also hold specific energies.

When you begin to incorporate shamanism into your life, it is beneficial to learn to infuse specific energies into objects, either by creating them or by energizing existing ones. We craft objects or create bundles (where a few items are 'bundled' together) for ceremony, to embody the outcome of shamanic journeys, to put on altars, to hold the energy of something we want to call into our lives, to burn so that we can release something, as gifts for spirit and much more. (In the following chapters I will sometimes suggest that you craft an object or create a bundle for a specific purpose.)

Such objects are always more than symbolic representations: they are containers of the energy and the spirit of the intent. That's what makes them powerful. Let's say you craft an object to call something into your life. This object holds the power of the focused intent you used whilst crafting, the spirit energy you asked to help and the energy of the ceremonial space in which you created the object. This enables it to form a bridge between the worlds, between the spirit and the material, between the intent and the manifestation of the intent.

An example with which you might be familiar is the Buddhist mandala sand paintings. If you have ever watched a monk create one, you will know that besides the painted symbols, what matters is the meditative focus, the intent and the prayers that are said whilst it is being created, not the actual sand painting as a piece of art. In fact, the moment it is finished, the monks destroy it, releasing into the world the energy they put into the mandala whilst creating it.

Exercise: How to create power objects

Creating objects or bundles which hold power in a shamanic sense requires intent, focus, time and spirit.

- Decide on your intent and find the materials that feel right (*some are suggested in the following chapters*).

- Call in spirit (*see page 46*).
- State your intent and focus on it throughout the crafting/drawing.
- Keep your focus, as this will help you to go into a 'creative trance'. Just craft or draw. Let it flow; don't interrupt.
- Meanwhile, keep asking spirit to be with you. State your intent again and feel it in the object. Really energize it with spirit, focus, prayer and intent.
- Hold the finished object for a while and again put your intent into it and ask spirit for help to place this intent in energetic form into this object.

Exercise: Turning an existing object into a power object

- No matter whether you have bought, been given or found the object, cleanse it in salt water and leave it to dry outside. Additionally, smudge it.
- Call in spirit; create sacred space.
- Sit with the object, holding it and getting a feel for its qualities. Let it speak to you. Listen with all your senses.
- Decide which intent this object should embody. Is it an object for healing, grounding or bridging (from the energetic field into manifested reality)? Is it to signify a certain direction on your altar or a particular concept, such as the feminine or masculine? Is it a dreaming object or a ceremonial one, able to be a container for various spirits?
- Formulate the intent and ask spirit to help you to infuse the energy of the intent into the object.

- Put it on your altar and leave it there for some time. Energize it in the same way a few more times before you begin to work with it. Cleanse it when it feels right.

When it comes to objects you buy, 'less is more'. Many people possess dozens of crystals and stones that have been blasted out of the Earth with industrial means for a mass consumer market. They pay little attention to them, piling them on shelves and mixing energies they do not understand. Not surprisingly, such objects have little power.

My soul-retrieval stone, mentioned above, is not pretty, but has been worked with and cared for over a long period of time. It has power.

When I worked with a shaman in Ecuador, I entered his healing hut one day when he wasn't there. I approached his altar and touched one of the big stones, which had caught my eye a few times. It almost threw me backwards. I had never felt a force like it in an object. Later, when I asked about the stone, I was told that it had been in the shaman's family for four generations, being passed from father to son. It was a 'normal' stone. What made it powerful was the intense spiritual work of four generations of shamans.

Chapter 6

The Shamanic Journey

Shamans have many ways of connecting with the spirit worlds and working with them. A good way to begin is via the contemporary shamanic journey, initially described by Michael Harner,[1] publicized extensively by Sandra Ingerman's books and utilized by most practitioners and people who use shamanic tools in their lives.[2] Most people use a rhythmic 'journey drumbeat', adjusted to the theta wavelength of the brain, to produce and maintain an altered state throughout the 20 to 30-minute journey. I have provided you with a download, which you can access via my website, www.christamackinnon.com. I advise you to use this whenever you journey.

Shamanic journeys lead to the upper, lower or middle worlds and can be used for many purposes. You can journey to connect with spirit allies and spirits in general. You can journey to find something you need to bring into your life, to retrieve split-off soul parts, ask for healing, reveal the root cause of an issue, discover solutions, receive advice, heal emotional wounding and/or find out about relationships.

You can also journey to receive teaching, guidance and learning about a range of issues, such as your task in this world, your shadow, your spiritual self, your higher self, your connection with your ancestors and much more.

Traditional and contemporary journeying

The traditionally initiated shaman travels out of the body whilst journeying and also has the ability to journey as somebody/something else, for instance an animal. I have journeyed countless times when practising soul retrieval for individual clients as well as in groups. During some journeys I was clearly in my body. On other occasions, I was out of body. However the journey unfolds is adequate, because it will lead you, in your own specific way, to the right place and the right outcome.

A contemporary shamanic journey is like a process that unfolds after you kick-start it with a clearly formulated intent and the use of your imagination. (*I outline the structure below and will give you examples in the next chapter.*) It will feel, especially in the beginning, like a deep altered state and a visualization.

Although you are asked to use your imagination, this doesn't mean that you need to be able to see clear images. Each of us functions primarily from a particular sense or senses: some of us are visually oriented; more kinaesthetic types sense and feel what's going on; others will hear things; some people are more intuitive and 'just know' what is happening. No matter if you are a feeling, seeing, hearing or intuitively knowing person, you can journey if you trust what comes to you.

State your intent repeatedly at the beginning of the journey, hold it as much as necessary throughout and state it again if you feel that you are getting somewhat lost, and you will find that the journey leads you to the requested outcome.

You will also be helped by letting the journey unfold in its own way rather than analyzing, questioning or manipulating it. In its entirety it will be consistent with your intent and meaningful to you.

The structure of a shamanic journey

A journey is always conducted in the same way. Here is the general structure. In the following chapters I will show you how to adjust it depending on your intent and whether you are journeying to the lower, upper or middle world.

- Prepare the room: light a candle, smudge or spray the space and switch off your phone.
- Clearly define your intent.
- Call in spirit (*see page 46*).
- Lie down or sit somewhere quietly. Switch on the drumming download (*see* www.christamackinnon.com).
- State your intent aloud a few times. Ask for spirit to help you with your journey.
- Now, whilst listening to the drumbeat, imagine that you are travelling down through tree roots, a passage, etc. (for lower-world journeys), or up via a rope, tree branches, clouds, mountaintops, etc. (for upper-world journeys), from your power place (*see below*). Use your imagination to kick-start the journey.

- After visualizing that you have travelled downwards or upwards, you might go through a transition phase leading you further down or up. In the upper world you need to go through layers; successive worlds will get hazier and more ethereal.
- From now on, let the journey unfold in its own way. Be aware, be curious, let it happen.
- If you get stuck or feel that you are losing your focus, state your intent again, breathe into your heart space and ask for help from spirit. Do not interrupt the journey.
- The journey will finish with a 'call-up'. The drumbeat will change and you will know that it is time to come back. Thank anyone you have met and come up from the lower world or down from the upper world.
- If you have journeyed to retrieve something, or if you have been given something by a guide or other helper, imagine bringing it with you.
- Thank spirit. Write your journey down.

Establish your place of power

So, now you are ready to do your first journey. This is to connect with your power place. Traditionally, the shaman's power place is a place in nature where they have had strong spirit experiences, heard their calling or been initiated, or a place which came to them whilst dreaming. It is a sacred place to which the shaman pilgrimages regularly to renew their spirit connection and to honour it. In some traditions, the place of power is also the place to which the shaman warrior returns when they are dying, to enter the spirit world when leaving the body for the last time.

In contemporary shamanism the place of power is in most cases initially established as an imagined place. In shamanic terms, this place, if set up and worked with in certain ways, is real and powerful, as it exists on one of the planes of reality, just not the material one.

The power place is where we feel that forces that we do not fully understand support us in our quests. For most people, it is represented by a nature scene. Generally speaking, it is the place from which we journey, the place where we connect with Earth and spirit and communicate with spirit allies, the place we visit when in need of guidance, sanctuary or restoration. It is also a place where we can 'plant' intents and dreams we would like to see manifest. Over time, your power place will be associated in your mind with the qualities it represents, and you can access its qualities at any given moment and work within it in many ways.

Exercise: Journey to connect with your place of power

- Prepare the room: light a candle, smudge or spray the space and switch off your phone.
- Clearly define your intent:

  'I am journeying to the lower world to find and connect with my power place. I ask spirit to help me.'

- Call in spirit (*see page* 46).
- Lie down or sit somewhere quietly. Switch on the drumming download.
- State your intent aloud a few times. Ask for spirit to help you with your journey.

- Travel down. You will arrive in a landscape. Observe it, explore it, get a feel for it. There might be a special area or place to which you feel drawn. Sit there for a while. This is your power place. You can change it if you wish by adding or removing things.
- When you hear the call-up beat, thank anyone you have met, come back and write the journey down.

Your power place is important. It is not static: it might change as you develop or you may change it deliberately over time, although the basic elements often stay the same. Mine has changed twice. It began as a place in Nepal, which is spiritually very important to me, but then it acquired some elements of a gorge in the Andes, where I had strong experiences during a mushroom ceremony, and lately a pyramid structure, which showed up during a retreat, seems to have established itself as a permanent fixture.

Connect with your spirit allies: power animals of the lower world

There is no shamanic work without spirit allies and teachers. These provide the shaman with power, wisdom, guidance, teaching and protection in the physical as well as spiritual worlds. Power animals are helping and guardian spirits best described as being 'the essence of a species perceived in the form of an animal'. They are essential for many tasks the shaman undertakes, such as lower/underworld journeys, healing, shapeshifting and soul retrieval. The relationship with them is central for the shaman, who strives for a strong, reciprocal relationship with all spirit allies.

Animal spirits are neither lifted to the status of deities nor lowered to the status of a psychological metaphor.[3] They are seen as manifestations of a natural power that is stronger, and often wiser, than human beings. When we are in touch with animal spirits, we are stronger and more likely to be in touch with our own nature as well as the natural world, and therefore less disconnected and fragmented.

In some cultures it is assumed that the spirits of at least two power animals stay with us from birth to keep us physically safe and healthy. Some shamans believe that losing a power animal is one of the causes of illness and they will journey to retrieve the power animal of a person who is ill. Certain North American indigenous cultures distinguish between four types of animal guide: journey guides accompany and help us through a certain part of our life's journey; messenger guides leave us as soon as the message is understood: shadow animal guides infuse us with fear, returning at times in our lives when we are severely tested; other guides stay with us over a lifetime.

Power animals are wonderful creatures. To connect and work with them is exciting and will enrich our life. Let me describe two of my 'lifetime' power animals to you and briefly outline my relationship with them.

> *My first journey with the intent to connect with a power animal led me to my power place, where a bear immediately came towards me. We were instructed to turn away a few times from the first animal we met, which I did. But the bear followed me and then she just took me in her arms, led me to a tree and held me very close. I felt a strong sense of warmth, love, comfort and*

safety. Next she took me by the hand and led me into a river, where we had a playful time together, which I thoroughly enjoyed.

This was at a point in my life when I was depleted of energy. The power animal showed me in no uncertain terms that I needed 'mothering' and more playfulness in my life. The bear has now been with me for almost 20 years.

An eagle connected with me later. He, too, has been with me ever since. He is quite fierce and focused, always pushing me forwards. He sees the bigger picture of my life and has, for instance, always been with me when I have gone through initiation rituals. He is often around when I want to give in to hesitation and fear. Sometimes he carries me to the upper worlds or flies with me to other destinations of a spiritual nature.

Whenever I do shamanic work I ask my power animals to be with me and help me. I could have never undertaken soul retrieval, for myself and for many clients, without this strong relationship with my power animals, especially with my bear, who has always been there, whatever grim landscapes and situations I have journeyed to. She has fought off attacking creatures, carried me on her back over water, cleared pathways in the underworld, showed me where to go in landscapes unfamiliar to me, and more than once rescued a hiding, terrified child and other parts of my clients, bringing them to me so that I could take them back to my clients.

It is important to recognize that we do not choose our power animal. It will come to us and it is for us to accept it, learn from it, work with it and build a relationship with it. All power animals are equal, as they are part of the energy of the divine in nature and our instinctual forces. They have thus certain qualities. Each provides a specific kind of medicine, which, let me assure you, will be exactly the one you need. For instance, a male participant in one of my groups who was very introverted and shy connected with a roaring black bear, whilst a woman who had real problems with her own femininity connected with an otter – a very feminine water energy – and a client of mine who was heavy and whose soul was starved connected with a hummingbird.

Although more than a psychological metaphor, power animals are also helpful in many ways psychologically: they are balanced creatures and having the energy of a power animal around will in itself help you with difficult emotional states because they are usually nurturing, loving, generous in their help and regard you positively. These qualities are in themselves healing forces.

It is difficult to describe the relationship with your power animal. You have to build it and experience it yourself. In comparison to spirit guides, power animals are not very verbal. Instead, they communicate by taking you to places and showing you things. They are not your instinct, but they certainly activate it. You don't have to do deep work or journey to get help and guidance from them. Just envisaging them and asking for help can produce astonishing results.

I live near Dartmoor National Park, a huge area of moorland, sparsely inhabited and in parts without mobile connection, where the weather can change very quickly. One day, during a hike, I found the weather closing in quickly, without much warning, and thick fog blocking almost all visibility. Moor landscape looks the same at the best of times, but without any visible landmarks, it is particularly easy to get disorientated and lost. I wandered around for an hour, getting tired, before I finally had to admit that I couldn't find my way back to the only road that would give me an idea how to get back to my car. So I closed my eyes, visualized my bear and asked her to 'lead me to the road'. I kept visualizing the animal walking in front of me, pointing the way; after about 15 minutes, I arrived at the road.

Exercise: Journey to meet your power animal

Use the drumming download and the journey outlined on pages 63–64 as a guideline and adjust the process as follows:

Your intent is:

> *'I am going to journey to the lower world to meet my power animal.'*

- Imagine that you are travelling down to the lower world.
- You will end up in your place of power, where you will meet an animal. Turn away from it. If you meet it repeatedly, ask it if it is your power animal.

- When you have met your power animal, let the journey unfold. Observe the animal – get to know its energy, its qualities. Be with it. Let it lead you.
- When you hear the call-up beat, thank your animal and ask it if it wants to come with you. If so, bring it with you, travelling up the same way as you travelled down.
- Thank spirit and your animal.

Integrating your power animal

There are many ways to integrate your power animal into your daily life. Write the journey down and also the qualities of the animal. Be with it often. Dance it, draw it, compose a song about it. Craft something or find something that represents it and put on your altar. Ask it to be there in all your journeys. Demonstrate its traits and qualities until they become part of you. However you integrate the energies of your power animal, as long as you develop a relationship with it, everything that feels right is okay.

I'm not exaggerating when I say that I have great respect and love for my power animals and I know many people who feel the same about theirs.

Connect with your spirit allies: upper-world teachers and guides

Not all schools of shamanism distinguish spirit guides or upper-world teachers from ancestral spirits, animal spirits and other spirits of the non-material invisible worlds. But, as the distinction between the upper and lower worlds gives us a structure, we can say that spirit teachers and guides are often seen as spirits of the upper world that appear to us in humanoid or symbolic form. They can be spirit entities that have been in a body, such as ancestral spirits, or that have never been in human form. As beings of the upper world, they are of a different vibration, having a mostly ethereal, cosmic quality, and their gifts have a quality of universal wisdom. They are the allies who can help us to see the bigger picture and who often answer questions, guide us, assist us and teach us about subjects concerned with soul, sense, purpose and meaning, but they also assist in healing, divination, ceremony and the energetic work we do in the different worlds.

Shamans often have several such allies, with different qualities, roles and functions. They can be acquired through journeying, plant journeys, initiation ceremonies, extreme altered state experiences or dreaming. Most importantly, as has already been emphasized, there can be no shamanic work without a strong relationship to spirit allies. I work with three upper-world guides whom I know quite well, but other guides show up at various times.

> *One of my teachers is quite stern and takes the form of a Native American. He is a no-nonsense, 'you haven't all the time in the world' kind of guy, who, together with the eagle power animal, forces me to keep the bigger picture in mind and stop wasting my time and energy with too much small stuff, which I have a tendency to do. He reminds me to push my limits when I get too comfortable. He is always there in ceremonial work and when clients face issues that require courage. He works through me in my energy-*

healing work and also during soul retrieval from the upper world. He isn't always ready to show me the way. He doesn't give me advice about trivial stuff, but lets me know – in no uncertain terms – that I am well capable of figuring it out myself. He has taught me quite forcefully that spirit teachers are not parents who do things for you and that you have to develop your own power and be responsible for your choices and the consequences.

Another of my permanent guides is a heart-centred female who has the spirit gift of expression in a gentle, soulful way. She was the first teacher who appeared to me and is more akin to my own nature. She reminds me of my own sacredness and beauty and those of everybody I work with. She shows me much symbolism when I work with clients and often also supports the people I work with in a holding, gentle way. She works with me and through me, especially with the feminine in women's groups and when there is emotional and soul wounding present. She always answers my questions. I meet her often when I dance, and my spirit soars, dancing with her in the skies. When we merge, which happens at times, we become one rainbow-coloured being and I feel whole, powerful and quite blissed out.

Guides are available to everybody. All you need to do to make contact with them is to be open and ask serenely. To have a power animal in place is in many cases enough to begin your shamanic work, but it is beneficial to learn how to communicate with upper-world teachers and to find an upper-world ally.

Exercise: Journey to meet your spirit teacher/guide

To meet a spirit guide you need to journey to the upper world. An upper-world journey feels different from a journey to the lower world. For some people, upper-world journeys are less clear, because the ethereal realms are unfamiliar to most of us. So it is essential to take your time.

Use the drumming download and the journey outlined on pages 63–64 as a guideline and adjust the process as follows:

Your intent is:

> *'I am going to journey to the upper world to meet a spirit teacher.'*

- Again, start in an imagined place or your power place and find a way to imagine travelling upwards. Be aware that you need to travel through layers and that the layers will often become increasingly ethereal and hazy. Let the journey unfold.
- You will meet teachers/guides in humanoid or symbolic form. Ask if they are your teacher/guide. When you have met your teacher/guide, be with them. Spend some time with them. Getting to know their qualities is important. You can ask them questions or ask for advice.
- At the end of the journey, thank the teacher or guide.

Integration work with your teacher

Afterwards, write about your journey and the qualities of your teacher/guide. Sometimes they will give you something symbolic in answer to your question or instruct you directly. Make sure you follow the advice or instruction. Put something that symbolizes your upper-world teacher/guide on your altar. To integrate them more, visualize them often, draw them, write about them and ask them for help and advice whenever needed.

Chapter 7

Psycho-Spiritual Work Between the Worlds

Now that you know how to journey and have connected to your spirit allies, you can begin to use journeying for your own healing, development and further connection to the spirit worlds. Journeying has many uses besides those already outlined in the last chapter. In fact, there are no limits to journeys that will assist your development, connect you with spiritual forces and help you to become whole.

As a general rule of thumb, journeys of a psychological nature lead to the lower world. Journeys that are undertaken to connect with higher spirit realms or ask for guidance from those realms usually lead to the upper world. Those to do with nature spirits and essences are middle-world journeys. In this chapter we will journey to the lower and upper worlds.

Here are some examples of intents you can formulate, stating the worlds and the helping forces you want around you:

- *Advice:* 'I am going to journey to the upper world to get advice about [insert appropriately]. I ask my power animal and spirit guides/teachers to help me.'
- *Finding the root cause:* 'I am going to journey to the lower world find the cause of my [for example, self-sabotage, depressive tendencies, anxiety, low confidence] and what would help me to overcome it/them.'
- *Retrieving for development:* 'I am going to journey to the lower world to retrieve whatever I need right now in my development.'
- *Retrieving specific parts:* 'I am going to journey to the lower world to retrieve [for example, my creative part, my playful inner child, my aliveness, my passion, the power of my anger or whatever I feel I have split off along the way].'
- *Letting something go/releasing:* 'I am going to journey to find out what I need to let go of to achieve [for example, more wholeness, peace, my potential].'
- *Learning:* 'I am going to journey to the upper world to learn about [my essence, my place of oneness, my task].'
- *Teacher and teachings:* 'I am going to journey to find a teacher who can teach me about [insert appropriately].'

Transformative journeys: retrieving, releasing, healing, developing

Preparation

In preparation for every journey:

- Define your intent clearly. If you are not sure which world to access, state both worlds and trust that you will end up in the right one.
- Open sacred space by calling in spirit.
- Always ask your spirit allies to help and accompany you on your journey.
- Use the format provided *on pages 63–64* and the drumming download.

The four transformative journeys below will give you some insight into what you might encounter when you journey, but rest assured there is no 'right' or 'wrong'. As long as you open sacred space, state and hold a clear intent, ask for help from your spirit allies and let the journey unfold, you can trust that it will be beneficial for you.

A journey of retrieval

All journeys of retrieval start in the lower world. We usually retrieve parts that we have split off on the way, such as our creativity, our playfulness, our anger, various inner child parts, our ability to make decisions or our confidence.

Here is an example of a journey that was rather complex and needed integration work afterwards (I will come back to this in the next chapter). I made this journey at the beginning of my shamanic work and have repeated it, with the same intent, a few times since. I would advise you to use this fairly neutral intent for your first journey. I will describe my journey in detail.

My intent

'I am going to journey to the lower world to retrieve something that I need right now for my development and to step into my power. I ask my spirit allies to help me and be with me.'

My journey

I am travelling down through my tree. At my place of power, my bear awaits me. She seems to be in a hurry, pulling me towards a mountain. At the mountain, we pass through an opening and crawl down a long passage. As it gets darker and colder, I begin to feel rather anxious. Situated at the centre of the mountain is a lake, which we need to cross. When I begin to step into it, the water sucks me down and, for whatever reason, I am unable to swim. There is no path around the lake. After waiting for some time, I state my intent again and ask for help. My bear suddenly grabs me, puts me on her back and swims with me across the lake. On the other side there is another passage. This time it is not only steep but also very slippery. I slide at great speed through the mud and arrive in an even darker space. I am on my own.

Sitting there in the mud, rather at a loss, I state my intent again and ask to be shown what I need to retrieve right now. Out of nowhere a jaguar appears, pushing me threateningly towards a chamber that I haven't been aware of until now. Way at the back sits a small girl, covering her eyes with her hands.

I walk towards her, but the closer I get the more she backs away from me, almost melting into the wall. This goes on for quite a while. I feel an overwhelming sense of sadness and loss when looking at the child, but can't reach her. I have no doubt that she represents a part of me, and as I slowly move closer I suddenly know that she left me during an accident. I remember my fear, the scream of my mother and the terror in my father's eyes when he saw me running across the road. I can hear the car's brakes screeching. This child is my courage, my fearlessness and my daredevil part, which has been hiding in this dark chamber deep in the mountain.

To cut a long journey short, the bear and I slowly and lovingly persuade the little girl to come with us. She is carried by my bear all the way back to my power place, where I hold her, talk to her, cry with her and finally laugh with her at the mimicry of my bear. I integrate her into my heart via a melting exercise.

A journey of releasing

Another journey I want to describe to you is one of letting something go. This can of course be something quite small, such as a habit, or it can be something substantial, such as certain people, anger you are holding on to or a part of you that is standing in your way without you consciously knowing it. Whatever it is, it is beneficial to do a journey because the journey itself will release it energetically and give you information about ways to release it in this material reality.

This example is from one of my students, Anne, who was journeying to release what was stopping her from entering fully into a relationship with a man. The journey took an unexpected turn and is interesting in its content as well as its outcome.

The intent

'I am journeying to the lower or upper world to find out what is stopping me from entering into the relationship I want and release it if necessary. I ask my power animals, guides and ancestral spirits to be with me and help me.'

The journey

Anne went down into her power place and from there she entered a stream, guided by a heron, one of her power animals. She tried to move forwards in the stream, but couldn't. Instead, she was pushed backwards. She tried to get out of the stream, but the current was too strong.

After what seemed a long time, she stated her intent again. A few minutes passed and suddenly she found herself in a cave, which she called 'the cave of the ancestors'. There she was told by a group of female ancestors that she needed to heal the wound in her womb, which was not hers but the wound of the female line she came from. Anne asked her ancestor how she could do this and was told that they would help her, which they did, right there and then, by filling the wound with different colours and herbs.

When it was done, they told Anne that she needed to 'let go of control'. She asked how she could do this and was told to 'dance herself free'. The ancestral women floated away and Anne found herself back in the stream. This time, she was facing the right way and swam back easily.

Physical healing

This is the journey of a client of mine, Stephen, who had experienced anxiety attacks and headaches over some months, which sometimes led to brief blackouts. The anxiety attacks, which were connected to him being a first-time father and feeling ill-equipped to take the responsibility for a family, had ceased over our time together, but the headaches didn't shift. He had undergone medical examinations, including a brain scan, which showed no physical cause, had been taking medication and had tried various complementary treatments without success. I introduced him to journeying more as a last resort and in the hope of getting some valuable information than in the expectation of a cure.

The intent

'I am journeying to the lower, upper or middle world to find out about my headaches and to receive the healing I need.'

The journey

Stephen's journey took a long time to unfold. When he had travelled to different worlds without getting anywhere with his search, I asked him to repeat the intent and sincerely ask again for spirit's help and guidance.

Finally a guide appeared and told him to look for his father, which fitted with his overall theme within the therapeutic process but was somehow strange because his father was still alive. The guide suggested that he travel back in time and Stephen found himself in a small dwelling isolated in the mountains of Nepal, where he, his brother and his parents lived. He whispered repeatedly, 'My father is dying because my brother and I need meat to survive.' Deep distress could be seen on his face.

The unfolding story was very touching. His father had sustained considerable injuries whilst hunting in icy conditions, which was usually avoided but had become necessary because the family was starving. Stephen described his mother's distress, his guilt and his fear of what would happen when the family was without a father.

At one point I urged him to ask his guide how this connected to his headaches. After a long silence he said, 'The guide and my father put their hands on my head and my father said, "Never be afraid to do what needs to be done for your children. They are the blessings of a man's life. Without you and your brother, my life wouldn't have been worth living. You are my blessing."'

Stephen was in tears watching his father's soul depart from the body and then, fairly suddenly, found himself back in my consulting room.

Stephen's headaches never returned after this journey. I don't know what exactly produced this miraculous cure. Was it the healing touch of the guide and father, or Stephen's new-found understanding that children were a blessing rather than a worry, or a past-life experience processed to an adaptive conclusion? What I do know, from experience, is that such unexpected and miraculous healing can occur and that rather than asking unanswerable questions, in shamanism we express gratitude for them.

Journeys of spirit connection, learning and developing

We journey to the upper world to learn, seek advice or connect. Journeys of learning or advice may be to learn about 'one-ness', 'my connection to spirit', 'my essence', 'my tasks in life' and more. Or we can journey with the intent of meeting a teacher and receiving advice, perhaps about a task or about the next step to take in our development. The journey that follows is one I took with the intent of seeking advice about my spiritual task.

The intent

'I am going to journey to the upper world to seek advice about my spiritual task in life. I ask my spirit allies and other helping spirits to accompany me.'

The journey

I journey upwards through the branches of my tree into the sky. Nothing happens for quite a while until I reach a rather thick layer of dense cloud, which it takes some effort to push through. I feel that I am getting lost. Nothing is in sight but hazy mists and swirling colours.

At last I reach a plateau on which my female spirit guide awaits me. I bow my head in greeting. She smiles gently at me and points upwards. We fly further up until we reach another plateau on which a circle of women seems to be waiting. I find myself in the middle of the circle. The women all chant, their eyes closed. I can see a flow of energy circling from one woman to another. My 'seeing' is getting stronger, but nothing is said. The women just keep chanting, moving their bodies gently.

After some time I become aware that the energy is now also extending from the women towards the centre of the circle, where I am sitting. One by one the women send out a stream of energy towards me until I turn into a rainbow-coloured being of great radiance. I feel an overwhelming sense of gratitude and bliss streaming through me, knowing that this is the 'shining of my wholeness'. This radiant rainbow-coloured being is me.

Next the rainbow colours turn into pure white light. I suddenly know that I am being shown my essence – that the colours of the rainbow are the visible layers of my underlying essence, which is pure white and indescribable.

> *Not a word is spoken until the end of the journey. Then, before the vision fades away, one of the women stands up. She is translucent in appearance, with white eyes and white hair. Her message is simple: 'Shine in all your colours and all will be well.'*

How to integrate your journeys

Journeys work on an energetic level and also partly on a cognitive one. It is vital to integrate their outcome and follow the advice you've been given during them. Sometimes, as in Stephen's example, no more work is needed, but most of the time it is advised. This doesn't mean intellectualizing the journey or interpreting it, but bridging the energetic reality and the material one.

How can you do this? Besides writing your journeys down in a journal, embodiment is a vital and powerful way to integrate your journeys. You can use movement and dance, crafting and ceremonial means (*see next chapter*). Here I will briefly use the journeys described above to show you how integration is done via dancing and crafting.

Integration through dance

Embodying the outcome of a journey through dance is a pleasant and profound way to encrypt on a cellular level. Dances that correspond to the outcomes of the journeys just described could be constructed in the following ways:

A dance with 'a retrieved part'

Holding the intent of 'welcoming and integrating this child part', I would put on some music, close my eyes and imagine being with the child. I would see her, feel her and, as this was a part which needed a lot of security and reassurance, I would hold her close and might talk to her as we danced. I would let the dance unfold, allowing images, feelings, sensations and movements to develop in their own way, whilst holding the intent of integrating this part into my being and into my life.

Anne's dance to 'let go of control'

Releasing something often produces rather strong movements. Dancing through any reluctance to let go (of control in this case or whatever it might be) and through any emotions that might surface, you can hold the intent of 'letting it go with love'. You can imagine it floating away, burning in a fire, being taken away by a stream, being buried in the earth or taken away by spirit allies. But, most importantly, let the body do the releasing by allowing the physical movements to unfold in their own way.

A dance of gratitude and healing

This can be any dance as long as the intent of 'gratitude' is being held. Express gratitude for the healing received and imagine carrying it into the future to reinforce it on a cellular level.

A dance of 'expressing my rainbow self'

I chose a chakra dance to work with the rainbow colours, visualizing that each chakra was shining brightly. It is interesting that when you focus on the chakras you can find out which ones dance themselves easily and where you feel blockages. I danced through images, sensations, memories and more that came to the surface, holding the intent of allowing myself to 'shine in all my colours'.

Integration through objects or paintings

For each journey outcome you can craft an object or draw a picture that holds the energy of the outcome. So, for the journeys described above, we would have four objects:

- an object representing the child part of the first journey
- an object representing 'letting go of control' for the second journey
- an object representing 'healing and gratitude' for the third journey
- an object or drawing representing my 'rainbow-coloured wholeness'

Releasing

Objects that hold the energy of something you need to let go or release need to be burned ceremonially or buried, or, if you live near a stream or the sea, to be taken away by water. Again, do this with intent and spirit. I will describe ceremonial work in the next chapter. Keeping the object, no matter how beautiful it is, is counterproductive, as the intent is to release something.

Manifestation

Objects that hold the energy of bringing something back into your life and objects that express gratitude should be placed on your altar and you should request that spirit help you to manifest this in your life. Treat the object in a respectful and sacred way, like all the other objects on your altar. You can also create a manifesting ceremony with the object, which I will describe to you in the next chapter.

Chapter 8

The Power and Beauty of Ceremony and Ritual

Ceremony and ritual form one of the cornerstones of both traditional and contemporary shamanic work. They can be generally defined as the sacred (and symbolic) enactment of intent. They are utilized for rites of passage and other transition work, for blessings, initiations, dedications, healing, divination and journeys to connect with the spirit world. They are also used for calling something into our lives or letting something go, for expressing gratitude, for questing for vision, for celebration, for honouring the ancestors, for bringing the community into harmony with spirit and much more. Well-constructed ceremonies bridge the many layers of our inner and outer realties, connecting us with universal powers, with spirit, with the divine and also with the multiple layers of our inner lives, such as our mind and body, and with something deeper, which we can call our soul.

In ceremony we can experience that the space between our everyday world and the world of our soul, between the mundane and the divine, is thinly veiled and that all the worlds are indeed interconnected and influence each other. Once we begin to feel that interconnection during ceremonial work, spending time in ceremonial space becomes truly magical and something within us balances effortlessly. Malidoma Somé, one of the African shamans I have worked with, echoes this by defining the purpose of ritual as a way 'to create harmony between the human world and the world of the gods, ancestors and nature.'[1]

Traditional ceremonies and rituals

There are many well-known indigenous ceremonies. Some are ritualized, consisting of patterns that have been repeated over generations; others are created afresh for specific occasions. Amongst the better-known ones are the sweat lodge ceremony, the pow-wow, the Navajo sand-painting healing ceremonies and the fire ceremony, which is found in variations all over the world. We have ceremonies to honour the cycles of life, such as the famous sun dance ceremony of the Lakota, which represents life, death and rebirth, and there are countless seasonal and moon-related ceremonies all over the world. In Africa particularly, we find very powerful ancestral ceremonies, whilst almost all indigenous tribes have ancient rites-of-passage rituals, such as the preparations for the 'walkabout' rite of passage in Australia's Aboriginal culture or the Navajo Kinaalda, a puberty celebratory ritual for girls. Plant medicine ceremonies to quest for healing, vision, knowing, guidance and illumination are used, for instance, by many shamans in South America, Mexico and Gabon. Trance dance ceremonies, where the shaman calls for spirit possession or shapeshifting, are also widely used in the Americas, Africa, Mongolia, Siberia and other Central Asian countries.

Many traditional ceremonies are prolonged affairs. The Gabonese healing and initiation ceremony takes at least 24 to 48 hours, and the sweat lodge ceremony takes from a few hours to a whole day and night. Vision quest ceremonies can take a few days and nights and the sun dance ceremony traditionally took a whole month but now takes place over four days.

There is also even more elaborate ceremonial work when the shamans, or parts of the whole tribe, make a pilgrimage to certain sites to perform ceremonial work to heal and re-balance our world, which is, according to tribal beliefs, increasingly and dangerously out of balance. The Mara'akames (shamans) of the Wixaritari (Huichol from Mexico), for instance, undertook an Earth renewal pilgrimage in 2015 that hadn't been attempted since the days of their ancient ancestors, travelling about 3,000 km (1,860 miles) to sacred sites to renew their old offerings to the land, the air, the water and the fire. They believed that these offerings were needed to spiritually redress the balance of environmental destruction and to revitalize the delicate connection between people and nature across the whole world.

The Kogi of the Sierra Nevada mountains in Colombia are also well known for their continuous ceremonial work to maintain the balance of the Earth, which, they state, would already have been destroyed without their ongoing ceremonies.

How ceremony works its magic

As already explained, in ceremony we enter into a sacred, symbolic enactment of intent. This intense enactment elicits powerful holistic responses within the individual psyche and the whole group participating, producing connection, healing, change and manifestation.

Here are a few pointers as to how ceremony works its magic:

- *Ceremony elicits holistic responses.*

  During a ceremony we drift effortlessly into an altered state of consciousness. We respond with our emotional brain by being moved. We reactivate cellular (or perhaps genetic) memories of how things were long ago. We also respond with our souls to the sacred field that is created through the ceremony, tuning into the wider fields around us.

- *It creates inner harmony and reduces inner conflict.*

  Holistic responses create harmony and reduce conflict in the inner world, and we know that such 'whole brain responses' can reach as far as to modulate alternative gene expression, facilitating profound healing.[2]

- *We enter a higher state of consciousness.*

  During ceremony we suspend the normal time/space continuum and enter fully into the present, a mental state in which all that matters takes place in the 'here and now'. This brings, as Sobonfu Somé, a female African ceremonialist shaman, formulates, 'all participants into a higher place of *consciousness within themselves*'.[3]

- *It has meaning for our inner world and helps us to manifest in outer reality.*

  During ceremony we create a powerful and meaningful story that expresses how, for instance, we want things to be; or what we wish for, or want to let go. Such meaningful stories and experiences shape how we see ourselves and, especially, how we dream and build our future, so affecting what we manifest.

- *Ceremonies and ritual create a powerful field.*

  Ceremonies and ritual connect and align the whole participating community, creating an energetic field and space where everybody is equally involved and immersed in a positive task. This field can become very powerful in itself, enhancing connection, harmony, healing and transformation for the group as well as for the individual.

- *They elicit a sense of being embedded in the transpersonal.*

  Everybody within a shamanic ceremonial space will experience, at least at one point, a connection with something bigger: they will sense and feel 'the sacred'. This will nurture a transpersonal sense of identity, beyond the isolated 'I', which is one of the desired outcomes of all spiritual work.

- *They contribute to creating a better world.*

  If we accept that there is an underlying energetic world, a timeless pool of consciousness into which we can tune and in which we can create, then we will understand that when we conduct a beautiful, harmonious and powerful ceremony, we are feeding dreams and experiences of beauty and harmony into this general pool. We are therefore contributing positively to this energetic field and consequently to the manifestation of more beauty and harmony in the visible world.[4]

How to create your own ceremonies

There are many ways of creating small ceremonies for yourself, although big ceremonies work best in groups, because the energy created by the group will enhance them. However you choose to do it, constructing a ceremony is a creative, enjoyable act.

You can use ceremonial work to celebrate something, to resolve an issue, to embody or let go of something, or to call something that you would like to manifest. You can give thanks via a ceremony, mark transitions, send out wishes and prayers, release fear, anger or grief and tune into and connect with the various aspects of yourself. Ceremonies can also be used to tune into, connect with and celebrate nature and various aspects of her, such as the seasons or cycles. No matter what the purpose, ceremonial work will support you in your quest for wholeness, connection and manifestation in the many ways I have outlined above.

How to structure a basic ceremony

- *Find the intent* and decide how you want to do the ritual (*there are examples below*).
- *Define the space:* I generally use stones to create a circle, marking the east, south, west and north. Anything that is available can be used as long as it

marks a sacred ceremonial space. The ceremony takes place inside the space.

- *Call spirit* and any additional spirits/powers you want to be with you during the ceremony. Ask aloud for blessings for the ceremony.
- *Create an altar.* A simple cloth on the floor will do, with a centrepiece that represents the intent of the ceremony. This can be a candle, flowers, a stone, a crafted object or whatever feels appropriate. When you put the object on the altar, state your intent aloud. Add something to represent the spirits you want to be present. I use fire, water, earth and air as well as something that represents spirit in general. What you use must relate to your intent and to the spirits you want present. The ceremonial shrine is the seating place of spirit during a ceremony.
- *Cleanse and protect the space* by walking around it with smudge or using sound in form of a Tibetan bell, singing bowl, drum or rattle.
- *The ritual.* Now perform the ritual. There are many forms, some of which will be described below. Use your imagination!
- *End the ceremonial work* when you feel it is done. Do something to mark the end (for example, drum, rattle, chant or meditate for a few minutes). Give thanks to the spirits. Next, clear the space – remove everything you used for the ceremony. Walk away! It's done. Go back to normal reality.

Create ceremonies for releasing, healing, manifesting and retuning

I will lead you through two basic ceremonies, the fire ceremony and the tree ceremony, which you can adjust and use for all the purposes described above, and then outline seasonal ceremonies and moon ceremonies for you so that you can retune to your natural rhythms.

It is important to understand that a ceremony begins the moment the preparations start. All preparations, such as crafting the offering and creating the shrine, are a vital part of the ceremony. They create the sacred space, intensify the intent, bring you into an altered state and connect you with spirit.

Exercise: The fire ceremony

This can be found with slight variations in most indigenous cultures around the world as well as in all contemporary shamanic groups and circles. I have participated in fire ceremonies in South America, North America, the Far East and various places in Europe. Although each was slightly different, all had the major ingredients in common. Here is a short version:[5]

- *Specify your intent.* The first step is to specify the intent of the ceremony, such as healing, letting something go, giving thanks, blessing, praying, calling something in, connecting with spirit.
- *Create the offering.* The burnable offering holds the energy of the intent (for example, what you want to let go of or call in). Use your imagination. What matters is that the object is constructed with complete focus, intent and spirit present (*as described in Chapter* 5).

- *Define the space, call spirit, create an altar and cleanse and protect the space* as described above. For a fire ceremony, you can build a fire outside or in an inside fireplace, use a candle in a bowl or buy a fire bowl for repeated use.
- *The ritual.* Whilst lighting the fire, you can again call in the spirits of the directions, ancestor spirits and guides and ask them to help you with your intent. Traditionally, either chants, rattles or drums or all of these are used to further connect with spirit. So, if you have any of them, use them. Put the offering on the fire whilst stating your intent aloud, with heart and focus. Watch it burn whilst holding your intent and sending it up to spirit. When the object has burned, put your hands through the fire, bringing the smoke first to your belly, then to your heart and then to your third eye.
- *Finish* the ceremony as suggested above.

Traditionally, fire ceremonies can take a long time, depending on the size of the community or group and how intense the ceremony becomes. In the Andes, for example, where three fires were included in the ceremonies I attended, they usually took three to four hours. An African fire ceremony I attended took most of the night, partly because the participants also moved around the fire, dancing themselves into a prolonged trance. As long as you don't rush ceremonial work, it doesn't matter how long it takes.

Exercise: The tree ceremony

This ceremony is a prayer ceremony. You may have come across it in various forms, as it is used on different continents. The best known may be the Buddhist prayer flags of Tibet and Nepal, which are based on shamanic traditions. I have also seen variations in Mongolia, North and South America and Africa.

This ceremony works beautifully inside or outside, alone or in a group. I have used it both ways many times. You can utilize it for almost any purpose, such as bestowing blessings, calling something in, remembering something with love, honouring ancestors, telling your story, sending out prayers and wishes or giving thanks. The nicest way to use it is around a theme, such as gratitude, honouring, blessing or prayer, because you can construct a prayer tree, keep it somewhere and add to it over time.

You need wool, cloths or ribbons in various colours and a tree outside or a tree-like plant or branches in a vase inside.

Let's say your intent is:

> *'To give thanks for all the blessings in my life.'*

- *Start:* Define the space, call spirit, create an altar and cleanse and protect the space as described above.
- *The ritual:* Put the tree, or whatever you are using, in the centre of your sacred space. Sit for a moment, meditate and contemplate your life. Find things you are grateful for, such as your friends, your job, your parents, your lover, husband, wife, child(ren), health, creativity or spirituality. Then, when you are ready, cut a piece of wool or cloth, walk around the tree and give thanks for one of these things by saying, for example, '*I give thanks for my health,*' and binding the cloth to a branch. Take another piece of ribbon. Walk around the tree. Say, for example, '*I give thanks for having a secure place of shelter in the world.*' Bind the ribbon to the tree. Take another piece of ribbon. Walk around the tree… Well, you get the idea. Do this until you run out of things to be grateful for. You will be astonished how many things there are.
- *Finish:* Sit in front of the branches/tree for a while. Meditate and send the gratitude out to the universe. You can drum or rattle a bit, or dance if you want to embody your gratitude through dancing. Thank spirit.

Clear the space and put the branches or plant somewhere to remind you of all the things you are grateful for. You can add ribbons or cloths with the same or other themes/intents at any time.

Seasonal ceremonies and moon ceremonies

Ceremonies that are based on the seasonal cycles as well as the cycles of the moon are very important in all strands of shamanism because they attune us to the rhythms and forces of nature as well as our own.

All basic aspects of ceremonies marking the beginnings and endings of nature's seasons use the sun as the marker of time. The sun rises and sets yearly along the horizon, reaching due east and due west at the equinoxes, and it rises and sets as far south and north as possible at the solstices. Ancient cultures saw these as the four primary solar gates and aligned with them through the places where they constructed their sacred sites (such as Stonehenge) as well as through their ceremonial intents. Reconnecting with the seasonal rhythms of nature through ceremonies at the equinoxes and solstices will not only reconnect you with your own natural rhythms but also attune you to the life-force and light-energy information carried by the sun into the body via those four solar gates.

- *Spring equinox:* At this time the length of day and night is equal all around the world. It is therefore about balance and also about 'sowing the seeds', i.e. releasing the old which might block us from moving forwards and bringing in the new by planting our intentions.

- *Summer solstice:* This is the longest day and the shortest night of the year. It is the first day of summer, when the great power of the sun can be experienced. Themes of the summer solstice are joy of living, the wonder and beauty of the Earth, the riches of everything in bloom, abundance, fertility, communication with spirits, rites, divination, sharing and enlightenment.
- *Autumn equinox:* Now the light shortens and the darkness grows. We move from the sun energy into the time of Earth energy, the time of darkness. Autumn equinox ceremonies are twofold. This is the time of harvest, when we give thanks for the fruits of past efforts. It is also the time of beginning to connect with and embrace the dark, the deep, the unconscious levels of ourselves and of manifest reality, to explore the riches therein and to practise introspection and being quiet.
- *Winter solstice:* This is the longest night of the year and the dawn of the returning light. Now begins the journey out of darkness into light. Traditionally, this is a time of releasing burdens and carrying them up to spirit to exchange them for blessings. It is a time to let go of old grudges and negative feelings, to forgive, to give thanks for the blessings of the year left behind and to call in the new, opening to the light of spring.

I often facilitate shamanic ceremonial groups at the solstices and equinoxes and the energy levels that are reached are usually very strong indeed and seem to produce some astonishing results. As the summer solstice in 2015 fell on a weekend, another shamanic teacher and I ran a long weekend of drumming, dancing and ceremony. One of the participants, Mary, had been invited (pushed really) by her daughter. She hadn't socialized for six months, in fact had hardly left the house, as she was grieving for her husband and deeply depressed. During the weekend she went through a deep healing process, released much of her sadness and also found her 'life-joy' again. She emailed me afterwards, thanking me profoundly and telling me that she had started to 'live again'.

One of the participants had never done anything like this before. After the night ceremony, she declared that for the first time in her life she had felt a connection to something mystical and magical, inside and outside. The difference in her was visible: she came alive.

How to create seasonal ceremonies

- *Intent:* Define your intent from the meaning of the season (*see above*).
- *Ceremonial space:* Set up the ceremonial space – preferably outside – and tune into the season. Add nature spirits and the spirits of the season to your calling. Let your body absorb the season. Moving, dancing, drumming, singing or chanting all intensify the connection. If you want to be even more elaborate, make a mask representing the season and wear it.
- *The rituals:*
    - ✧ *Releasing:* You can make a 'release bundle', which consists of binding together different items that you want to release, or release everything you want to release separately. Then use the fire ceremony

described above, or bury the items, or find a stream and let them float away.

- *Sowing the seeds:* You can either literally sow some seeds outside or in a pot, holding the intent of what you want to bring into your life. You can also plant your intentions by creating something, or construct a board, or make a collage, or use the tree ceremony described above. Keep whatever you have created.
- *Celebration:* Do something that really celebrates the summer. Make something very colourful that expresses your joy and gratefulness. Dance a lot – the crazier, the better. Thank spirit profoundly. Tune into the strong light of the sun, feel it and try to get the messages it is sending. Remember, you are doing this on a solar gate day.

However you create your ceremonies, tune into the season fully. Absorb it in your body as well as your heart and mind. The intent is to get in tune with it, then let whatever you have done gestate and manifest.

How to create moon ceremonies

Monthly cycles use the moon as the marker of time. Reconnecting with the cycles of the moon will tune you into the feminine, the flow of the wild, nurturing, intuitive, heart-centred, life-giving and sustaining force, and the monthly cycle of releasing and beginning.

Working with the moon is of course best done outside at night. The moon asks us to listen, to absorb, to intuit and to express creatively. When carrying out the ceremonies, use your imagination. Be creative.

- *Full moon* is a time of releasing all that which no longer serves us, such as addictions, hurtful relationships, anger, fear and emotional pain or obstacles in our paths. Release them with your blessings. You can craft objects or draw or write and then create a fire ceremony for releasing. You can go outside and express what you want to release: dance it away, howl it away, bury it.
- *New moon* is for new beginnings, for manifestation, birth and rebirth – all cycles that will be completed by the full moon. Set intentions. Write them down, make a board, sow seeds in a pot. Things need time to gestate. Go outside if you can and ask the moon to help you gestate whatever you want to give birth to.

Chapter 9

Dancing with Spirit

There is no doubt that our tribal ancestors around the world loved to dance and that people of all cultures, especially their shamans, healers and medicine people, used – and still use – ecstatic dancing as a spiritual practice. Gabrielle Roth, the urban shaman and creator of the 'Five Rhythms of the Soul' dance sequence, expressed this beautifully when she wrote:

> *'... in the beginning we all danced... Our ancestors danced until they disappeared in the dance, till they felt the full force of spirit unleashing their souls. This was [their] religion, and it was ecstatic and personal and tribal and it moved through time like a snake. Until it found itself in the wrong garden.'*[1]

The trance dances of tribes or shamans are fascinating to watch and to experience, although they can be long ceremonial affairs, usually for the benefit of the whole community.[2] I have watched and participated in traditional trance dance ceremonies in various parts of the world, and for me, trance dance has become one of the most wonderful ways of entering an altered state, journeying to the spirit world and releasing control, so that the dancer disappears and becomes the dance. This kind of dancing enables the unhindered flow of energy through my physical and energy bodies, balancing and healing them in the process. I often receive teachings when I dance and I generally experience a blissful state of being that is beyond mind and connect with what I would call my 'essence'.

Traditional trance dance

Traditionally, ecstatic dance is used to enter non-ordinary states of consciousness, to connect and communicate with the spirit worlds and to work within them. It is used for balance between humans and spirit, the body/mind and soul/spirit, for vision, initiation, healing, transformation and celebrations of various kinds. From the sun dances of the peoples of the North American Plains and Canada to the whirling dances of the Sufis, from the Umbanda trance dances of Brazil and the wild, ritualistic dances of the shamans of Siberia and Mongolia to the masked dancing of the Balinese and the depiction of the Hindu god Shiva as a dancer, trance dance has a spiritual component. The Inuit drum and dance ceremonially – the bear dance is one of their better-known dances – and so do all remaining tribes of Africa. The voodoo trance dances and spirit possessions of Haiti are thought to date back 6,000 years. The ghost dances of the Sioux, the Salish spirit dance on Vancouver Island, the ecstatic peyote dances of the Huichol of Mexico and the Mongolian and Nepalese shamanic journeys to the spirit worlds all involve intense trance dancing, with drumming as well as song and chanting.[3]

In some cultures, especially in those where participants dance in circles, the steps of the dancers are ritualized (for example, in the Huichol deer dance or peyote dance), but whether the dances are ritualized or not, the drums will be beating over long periods of time, with the beats becoming faster when ecstatic levels are reached, and other instruments can be brought in, too. If shamans are dancing for purposes such as divination, prophecy or healing, they also often use their voices, singing and chanting spirit songs to connect or to convey messages from spirits. Fights with malicious spirits may also be expressed during the trance dance of the shaman, for instance for the healing of a person or the community, or if the shaman has to extract a spirit who has possessed the body of a community member.

Trance dance is used in many cultures to facilitate spirit possession, meaning that the shaman will be 'possessed' by the spirits during the dance. African shamans often aim for spirit possession, and some shamans from other parts of the world, such as South America, Mongolia and Siberia, work in this way. There is a distinct change in the dance when this happens, as the shaman opens themselves up to become a vessel for a spirit, which will enter their body and mind and express itself directly through movement and voice. Strong spirit possessions achieved and expressed through trance dance are dramatic affairs. They are not for the faint-hearted, but, if genuine, they show the extreme abilities of traditional shamans.

Contemporary adaptations: dance yourself awake and free

Trance dance

Trance dance has become a phenomenon all over the world, especially since electronic dance music, which is based on rhythms of 120 to 180 beats per minute (depending on genre), arrived on the music scene in the late 1980s and the 1990s. The beats are comparable to the drumbeats that are used to induce trance states in shamanism. A vast dance festival and clubbing scene has emerged since then, with drugs enabling people to dance all night. This shows us how much we all yearn for the experience of 'trance and dance' denied to us since we 'found ourselves in the wrong garden', where free expression of the body was increasingly declared 'sinful'. This contributed to keeping us on non-spiritual, restricted level of consciousness we are on today. Shamanic trance dances are powerful tools for changing this. They enable us to expand our consciousness, remove our ego barriers, let our body flow and express itself, embody all sorts of things, move stuck energies, feel our blissful, ecstatic essence and more.

Contemporary shamanic trance dance

Contemporary practitioners have adapted shamanic trance dance in many ways, all aimed at healing our relationship with spirit by connecting with our inner essence and at mental, emotional and spiritual healing and transformation.

In shamanic trance dance, we go on an inner journey during which, according to Wilbert Alix, one of the people who brought traditional trance dance to the West, our ego personality disappears and we become more like 'our spirit'.[4]

Whilst dancing is great fun, moves energies, allows self-expression, lets the body's natural rhythm take over and contributes to our spiritual development by connecting us with deeper layers of ourselves, it also has mental, emotional and physical health benefits. According to research at the Albert Einstein College of Medicine in New York, elderly people who danced frequently had a 75 per cent reduced risk of developing Alzheimer's, reduced rates of stress and depression and increased levels of energy and serotonin. Dancing improved their strength, flexibility and balance, boosted their cardiovascular health, increased their cognitive capacity and created new neural pathways in the brain.[5]

Contemporary shamanic trance dance is performed in groups, in a sacred ceremonial space and with spirit being invited. There is a preparation phase and each individual dancer will formulate the intent of their dance. Usually the facilitator works together with a group of drummers, who use various drums, led mainly by African *djembes*. It can be done with recorded music, but a group of good live drummers works magic because they can take the dancers up and down, adjust to the energy in the room and also create an energy field that will support the dancers.

I have facilitated many trance dance groups. We always have a day of preparation and the dance begins in the evening and lasts until all participants have danced. A dancer usually dances between one and four hours before they fall down or just stop and stand still. I have two to four people looking after each dancer. They group themselves around them to keep them safe, making sure that they don't bump into anything, or into other dancers, and catch them when they fall. This enables the dancer to close their eyes and let go completely. The dancing may start with a breathing technique called 'the fire breath' or I may whirl the dancer before they begin.

To illustrate how profound the experience can be, here is the account of Jan, who participated in one of my trance dance groups:

> *This experience happened near the beginning of my interest in shamanism and was partially responsible for my increasing journey into my spiritual self. I attended a weekend workshop which involved an evening of trance dance with drumming. During this an individual stood in the centre of a group of four other people, who acted as the safety boundary for the middle person. They then danced to live drum music, with their eyes closed, until they tranced out and safely fell to the floor.*
>
> *When it came to my turn, I remember being conscious of the drumbeat for a while until it became a part of me. It felt as though the drums were me and the music was me, and I lost total awareness of my surroundings and, in a sense, of myself. Then a void opened up and I could see and sense the whole cosmos. I was standing on the threshold of an amazing place and all I had to do was step into it and become one with it. I can recall the moment when I stopped. It felt as though all my molecules separated and my body elongated and became one with the universe, to which I was fully*

connected: I was one with the cosmos and everything in it, and my concept of life changed. I then recall being aware of lying on the floor.

For me, this experience opened up an ever-increasing interest in my spiritual self and a conscious decision to explore and understand this part of my life more fully.

Five Rhythms: dancing the wave

Gabrielle Roth's Five Rhythms Dance, which she described as the practice of a moving meditation of ecstatic dance, has become a worldwide practice. Gabrielle, a remarkable woman and urban shaman who combined shamanic ecstatic trance dance, Eastern philosophies and contemporary dance movements, trained many facilitators all over the world. She described the practice of Five Rhythms as a soul journey, because by moving the body, opening the heart and freeing the mind, we could connect to the essence of the soul, the source of all inspiration, possibilities and potentials.

The five rhythms form a wave:

Flowing: Fluid movement – you feel out where you are and get into your own body.

Staccato: Short, sharp moves – you confront the space and begin to be in it.

Chaos: Chaotic moves – you let go completely, release what you are holding and surrender to the wildness of your body.

Lyrical: Light and gracious, a subtle continuation of letting go - you are now in the space to really dance.

Stillness: You drop into the essence of the dance, into being the dance, into the still point within yourself.

Dancing the Five Rhythms produces remarkable results. The rhythms move you, in a semi-structured way, through whatever is happening, through whatever you are feeling, moving it energetically, without suppression, into a state of stillness. I have shed tears, become furious and felt heavy as well as blissed out with sheer joy. It is an amazing practice and I am sure that you will find a teacher and group near you. Try it. It is ideal if you want to start dancing as a psycho-spiritual practice.

Chakra dancing

Chakra dancing is very much inspired by tribal and spiritual dancing from different regions around the world. It blends free-flowing movements with specific frequencies of beats and sounds, each connected to one of the seven underlying energy centres of the body and to certain images. For instance, the rhythms of the base chakra are inspired by tribal dancing as found in the indigenous cultures of Africa, Australia and North America, as well as in the natural movements of animals. Together with images such as dancing around a campfire or imitating the movements of an animal, they help us to get into our base energy, to activate it, clear it and move it through the body.

Chakra dancing is generally based on the idea that emotional, mental, physical and spiritual blockages are stored in the cells and muscles of the body and show up as images, memories, hunches, feelings, intuitions and aches and pains. Dancing through the vibrations of the seven centres gives them a chance to be released. It is interesting that archetypal images connected to the chakras - animals, warriors, goddesses - often show themselves to dancers, even without being suggested. And in most cases, once we reach the crown chakra, we feel a strong spiritual connection to the wider fields of existence.

I have facilitated chakra dancing for groups of women and have often chakra danced myself. Even if we have stuck energies, aching bodies and emotional issues, chakra dancing is a magical medicine and produces much joy. I would encourage you to try it, especially if you like a bit of structure when you begin to dance.

Chakra dancing, Five Rhythms dancing and shamanic trance dancing are all spiritual paths and practices that lead to wholeness. They therefore should not be a one-off practice. The more often you dance, the more beneficial you will find it.

Dancing the shamanic journey

Another way of using dance in your practice is to dance the shamanic journey, either alone or in a group. You can either use a drumming download or you can drum whilst journeying. The space needs to be set up ceremonially, spirit must be invited and a clear intent stated. Then, instead of sitting still or lying down to travel to the upper or lower worlds, you dance. The body moves whilst the mind becomes aware of images, feelings, insights, sudden knowing and more, until the journey reaches its completion.

The advantage of dancing the shamanic journey is that the body is involved, so you are also shifting energy on a physical level throughout the journey.

Dancing for integration, merging and embodiment

Dance is also a means of embodying any intent or spirit or essence physically, on a cellular level. I talked about this in Chapter 7, when using dance to integrate the outcomes of journeys. Besides dancing to embody these outcomes, you can also dance intents, power animals, guides and all essences. Hold the intent, imitate the movements of the animals, be the animals in your dance. Really feel it and you will connect with something quite profound as you let the dance unfold.

If you want to merge with an element, be it earth, water, air or fire, again you can dance it. Hold the intent, imagine that you are becoming the element and feel its movements, its power. Again, let the dance unfold.

Chapter 10

The Medicine Wheel

A wonderful map, ceremonial construct and teaching tool is the medicine wheel, which depicts all of life in cycles and circles, along with how its aspects work together. Circle-like structures have been used all over the world as ways of depicting, organizing and passing on information about the world and as ceremonial spaces to honour life and spirit. The mandalas of the East, the Mayan and Aztec circles of South America, the Neolithic stone circles of Europe and the circles in Australian Aboriginal and New Zealand Maori traditions are just some of the many circles that speak of life in cycles.

The medicine wheel, also called the sacred hoop, is used by indigenous peoples of the North Americas but, as most sources state, comes originally from the Maya in South America. 'Medicine' doesn't mean something that medicates, but is a term used in those indigenous traditions to describe the mysterious power inherent in everything and everybody – a unique quality.

The medicine wheel is, like all ancient wheels, based on nature observation, and it moves from the elegantly simple – a centre and four directions – to the increasingly complex, with the number of wheels being theoretically infinite. In its many adapted forms it is now also widely used as a tool for personal exploration and development, with most contemporary practitioners using eight directions around the wheel and a split centre. Wheels are applied to a wide variety of subjects, such as the workings of the wider universe, Earth and nature, communities and the humanity within the whole. There are also wheels about specific human aspects such as the body, thoughts, emotions, beliefs, behaviour, creativity, spirituality, development, relationships and more. It is believed that we all carry the 'sacred hoop of life' within us and thus the medicine wheel resonates with us on a deep level.

The powers of the four directions

The basic formation of the medicine wheel is based on the four compass directions – east, south, west and north – and represents the powers of those directions as well as their interrelatedness. These four directions correspond with the four elements, the four seasons, the four races of humanity, the four aspects of the human (the mental, physical, emotional and spiritual) and the four stages of life (birth, childhood, middle age and old age/death).

In the centre we find 'the children's fire', representing the infinite sacred mystery, which always was and always will be.

If we add four more directions, we have the ancestors in the southeast, our dream of life in the southwest, rules and laws (karma) in the northwest and our design of energy in the northeast.

The basic wheel connects the directions in a circle (the feminine) and also connects them via the spirals (the masculine) that extend from the centre.[1]

The medicine wheel

Exercise: Connect with the powers of the four directions

There are countless ways to work with the basic medicine wheel, but all wheel work requires that you call in spirit, have a clear intent, open your heart, ask for guidance and then trust whatever comes to you.

The following is a good exercise to start exploring the sacred powers of the wheel. It is best done outside, but you can do it inside if you live in an urban environment.

- *Create a wheel.* Use four stones or crystals or the items from your altar. Place them in the directions of the east (fire), south (water), west (earth) and north (air), leaving enough space to stand in the middle of the circle.
- *Call in spirit*, whilst standing in the middle of the circle. Still yourself.
- *Turn east* and say:

    'I ask the spirits of the east to teach me about the sun and fire and how to bring the sacred of the east into my life.'

- *Turn south* and say:

    'I ask the spirits of the south to teach me about water and the plant kingdom and how to bring the sacred of the south into my life.'

- *Turn west* and say:

    'I ask the spirits of the west to teach me about earth, about the deep mother and how to bring the sacred of the west into my life.'

- *Turn north* and say:

    'I ask the spirits of the north to teach me about air and the animal kingdom and how to bring the sacred of the north into my life.'

Stay in each direction for as long as it feels right and just let the teachings come to you. You will get much information and insights in the form of feelings, images and advice.

Make sure you write down what you remember afterwards and find ways to bring the sacred of each direction into your life.

Finish by thanking all the spirits and then dismantle the wheel.

The human aspects of the wheel

The medicine wheel addresses all aspects of the Self: the conscious aspects and the more unconscious aspects of our ego self, the dark and the light aspects of our psyche, and our soul and spirit aspects. We generally work with the wheel with the aim of integrating the aspects to the highest possible extent at any given moment. We can also use it to look at our development at each stage in our life and our connections to universal fields.

The following descriptions of the directions will provide a basis for you to work with:

- *The east* is the place of the sun, the place of birth, death and rebirth. It is associated with spirit, vision, illumination, creativity and the upper world. The east asks us to look at our spirituality.
- *The south* is the place of water, of our emotional self, of the inner child, with its beauty, innocence, playfulness and wonder but also its wounding. The south asks us to look at our emotional self.

- *The west* is the place of earth, of the Earth, the physical world. It is the place of our human body, and for our psyche it is the place of 'shadow', the underworld and our Earth soul. The west asks us to be introspective, to go deep and confront and transform our own darkness, but also to retreat and dream.
- *The north* is the place of air. It is cold and dark. Humans need skill, knowledge, endurance and wisdom to thrive in the north. It is the place of the mental faculties, the place of the adult. The north asks us to 'stop the world', examine our thoughts, philosophies and beliefs and grow wise before we die.

Exercise: Getting a snapshot

This is a basic but very effective exercise to tune into the four major aspects of yourself: the emotional, child self (south), the physical/manifesting self (west), the mental, adult self (north) and the spiritual self (east).

- *Create a wheel.*
- *Call in spirit* and centre yourself.
- *Turn south.* Ask:

  'Which image represents the south for me? How do I feel in the south? What is my task right now in the south? Is there anything that needs changing in the south?'

- *Turn west.* Ask:

  'Which image represents the west for me? How do I feel in the west? What is my task right now in the west? Is there anything that needs changing in the west?'

- *Turn north.* Ask:

  'Which image represents the north for me? How do I feel in the north? What is my task right now in the north? Is there anything that needs changing in the north?'

- *Turn east.* Ask:

  'Which image represents the east for me? How do I feel in the east? What is my task right now in the east? Is there anything that needs changing in the east?'

- *Centre:* Let it all go. Stay for a while in the centre and experience the calmness there. Whilst the wheel of life is turning, you can stay calmly in the centre.
- *Finish:* Write down what you remember. Thank spirit. Dismantle the wheel.

This exercise lends itself to a second round:

- Travel around the wheel again and ask in each direction: 'How can I change what needs changing?'
- Again, come back to the stillness in the centre at the end.

Going deeper

You can ask many deep questions in the directions. As long you set the wheel up in a ceremonial way, with focus and spirit present, you will get answers. Here are examples of some profound questions:

- *East:* 'For what service/purpose has spirit given birth to me?'

- *West:* 'How do I manifest this?'
- *South:* 'Which emotions do I need to bring to the fore to achieve this?'
- *North:* 'Which work would best align me with spirit's intent for me?'

The circle and the diagonals

The circle

The directions on the wheel are connected via a circle, which is a developmental map where we travel from birth (east) via our childhood (south) to middle age (west) and old age (north). From east to west our life's journey is often fairly unconscious – we are born, go through childhood, education, youth and find a job, partner up, have children – then we hit the west, where we encounter the so-called 'midlife crisis'. The west asks us to turn inwards and become conscious of our life's path, creating meaning and purpose and including the spiritual. If we don't do this, we won't reach the wise north and will lead fairly meaningless lives from that point onwards.[2]

We also go through this journey daily, with every task we undertake. If we take a snapshot of where we are and what's going on with every task, we will often find that we are getting stuck in the emotional south, not growing through the introspective west and are therefore unable to complete in the north. We have all experienced this: we have an idea in the east and begin to work at it until our wounded, insecure, emotional south bombards us with self-doubts and anxieties and is immediately supported by our unsorted north with negative thought processes. This is where we usually stop and the idea never manifests in the west or completes in the north. Or we find that we are well developed in one direction, but lacking in another: we may have many ideas in the east, for example, but lack the discipline of the 'wise adult' in the north. Or we have a great work ethic, but lack the passion of the south and the creative drive of the east. All such issues can be addressed via the wheel.

The diagonals

The diagonals of the wheel are balancing opposites consisting of two axes:

North/South

North/south is the personal axis. The intelligent, thoughtful, skilful adult needs the emotional, playful, delighted and wondrous child, and vice versa, to achieve balance. The emotional south, disconnected from the cerebral adult in the north, can be self-indulgent and a prisoner of its own emotions, whilst the north can become hard and judgemental without the emotional self from the south.

East/West

East/west is the spiritual axis. The east is illumination, ascent, inspiration, creativity and spirit. The west is the physical, shadow, introspection, descent and the Earth soul. Without the west, the east is directionless spiritual energy or can be ungrounded, self-serving and egocentric spirituality, because the introspection and shadow work in the west has been neglected. Without the east, however, achievement in the west can be meaningless, dissatisfying and based on hollow material aspirations.

We can explore, connect and balance all human aspects with the wheel. I love teaching and working with it.[3]

Chapter 11

Spirit, Soul and the Sacred in Nature

Living in a predominantly urban world, it is easy to forget that shamanism derives from communities that were deeply embedded in the natural world, observed it closely and were connected to its spirits and the Earth's soul. This is a big subject in shamanism, to which I cannot do justice in this book. That said, there can be no shamanic practice without the connection to nature and the deep knowing that we are an integral part of it because we are both planetary and cosmic beings. I will therefore concentrate on the sacred in nature and the connection between our souls and the natural environment. I will also introduce you to some basic tools that will enable you to reconnect to both nature and your own nature.

An Earth-based traditional cosmology

People all over the world who are still rooted in Earth-based traditions or connected to them have always maintained that being embedded in nature means being close to creation, the creator and the divine. In shamanic cosmology the sacred is directly experienced through creation and can be understood through observation and communication with the spirit(s) of nature.

From a shamanic viewpoint, everything in the web of life is not only alive and interrelated but also sacred, as it derives from the same spiritual field. Humans, albeit complex, are one of the manifestations of this field, but not a superior species. This is a knowing we have lost, and it has led to devastating consequences. The more we define ourselves as 'separate' from nature, the less we follow the intent of the spiritual dimension from which we have arisen and the more we harm not only the manifest dimension of our Earth, which we can see in the ecological damage we have done, but also the spiritual and sacred dimension of the Earth and ourselves. It is therefore not surprising that we hear increasingly urgent calls from shamans, medicine people and tribal leaders to wake up to the dangerous level of our disconnection from the sacred in nature and our violation of her inherent laws.

For many generations we have been led to believe that the divine is somewhere 'out there', but in fact we will – with some focus and engagement – find it 'right here'. The Aboriginal teacher and artist Miriam Rose Ungunmerr-Baumann, who has received an honorary doctorate for her work, expresses this when she writes that it is easy for her to experience God when she hunts, is in the bush or is amongst trees, as her people have been so aware of nature that it is natural for her to feel close to the creator.[1] And Carlos Perez Shuma, a Peruvian shaman, echoes this from the other side of the world when he says,

'...because in nature there is God and God talks to us in our visions.'[2]

This knowing of the divine in every living thing leads inherently to everything in nature being treated with respect, rather than being exploited for the gain of one species, namely our own. This doesn't mean, however, that Earth-based cultures are sentimental about animals and plants. Animals are killed for food and plants are eaten, but understanding their inherent spirits leads to an honourable way of taking their lives. When I was in Mongolia I was touched by how the nomadic herders, whose livelihood was rearing and slaughtering animals, honoured their spirits. You could find animal skulls everywhere being used to house the spirits of the slaughtered animals. Societies that are still Earth-based will also thank the animal spirits for giving their earthly body for human nourishment and often hold ceremonies in honour of them. When I worked with shamans in South America, no food was consumed without offerings to the spirits and all leftover food was given away rather than binned. When they cut plants for healing or collected wood for a ceremony, they always left an offering in return and thanked the trees and the plants. In most traditions, including the North American, Inuit and Siberian, all edible parts of the animal are eaten, spirit guides are asked to lead the hunters to the animal spirit to thank it, and feathers, skins and furs are worn in ceremony. The contrast to our cruel factory farming and slaughtering of about 56 billion animals per year worldwide couldn't be stronger.

Once we reconnect to the divine in nature and begin to feel it, we will also understand that sustainability is directly connected to this and appreciate the shamanic notion that nature teaches us right from wrong. Eli Gatoga, a Cherokee chief, expressed this when he said, 'The Indian made an effort to know of spiritual things from his own observations of nature, because all truth can be found in Nature.'[3]

The right way to live is in balance and harmony with the natural laws that are inherent in the underlying field of the divine mother. This means respecting the sacredness of all life, giving something back whenever we take something, honouring the spirits within nature, contributing positively to the underlying energetic spiritual field and striving to live in a way that sustains all creation.

Our current spiritual beliefs, based on our religions, do not support this right way of living, as they affirm human superiority instead of equality, guardianship and the sacredness of all living things: 'God blessed them and said to them, "Be fruitful and increase in number; fill the earth and subdue it. Rule over the fish in the sea and the birds in the sky and over every living creature that moves on the ground."'[4]

The contrast to indigenous teachings is strong. Here are just a few examples: Slava Cheltuev, a shaman from the Dyayat Kypchak clan of Russia's Altai mountains, says: 'Our earth is sacred ... living on the earth, each person must respect their place. We must respect it, protect it and it will give us life, it will give us health.'[5] At the international Indigenous Leadership Gathering 2014, two of the four agendas had sustainability and sacredness at their heart, and Oren R. Lyons, university professor, author of many books and Faithkeeper of the Turtle Clan, pulls it together stringently:

'In the absence of the sacred, nothing is sacred. Everything is for sale.'[6]

The starving of our sacred Earth souls

Shamans believe that within this interconnected web, the harm we do to nature, we do to ourselves, especially to our souls. My own observations as a psychologist, therapist and shamanic practitioner over many years have shown me how much disenchantment, emotional and mental imbalance and rootlessness modern people experience. If we look at human development, we realize that we are indeed beings of both nature and culture, and that our increasing neglect of the nature dimension of ourselves causes soul starvation and mental/emotional problems. This is supported by profound research which also shows us the healing power of nature on the psyche. Nature symbolism is, for instance, dominant in healing experiences and people of all age-groups feel emotionally more stable, more peaceful, more alive, more compassionate and re-enchanted after spending time in nature.[7]

Nature also shows us alternatives to our consumer-orientated way of life. Bill Plotkin, a shamanic eco-psychologist who facilitates long, intensive wilderness camps, observes that:

> *...healthy human development requires a constant balancing of the influences and demands of both nature and culture... By suppressing the nature dimension of human development... industrial growth society engenders an immature citizenry unable to imagine a life beyond consumerism and soul-suppressing jobs.*[8]

Unfortunately our longing for nature is increasingly pushed into the subconscious. Only when we are encouraged to dig a bit deeper do we realize that shamanic teachers are right: our mind still associates being powerful, being at home, feeling safe, peaceful and healthy, with being in nature. In my practice I have never experienced anybody who, when asked to find their place of power, sanctuary, peace or healing visualized a crowded city, their place of work, a shopping mall or club or any other place in our urban world. People of all ages and social backgrounds visualize a place in nature.

The connection to nature is not only important for our mental and emotional wellbeing but also for re-experiencing the sacred within ourselves. As we begin to reconnect consciously with nature, we recognize that our Earth soul is wild and needs to be allowed to tune into where it lives, namely the vast and beautiful realms of nature, in order to be nourished and reflect itself back to us. In shamanism, every time we connect with nature in a sacred way, we reinforce the sacred within us, nurture our soul and give ourselves a chance to experience 'being home'.

Contemporary shamanic nature work and tools

Shamanic practitioners, both contemporary and traditional, will spend time in nature to be alone and still and to converse and merge with nature spirits, allies and helpers. They will learn from nature, be inspired by it, heal and do healing work with the underlying energy fields, revitalize and re-energize their powers, quest for vision, tune into the seasons, reconnect with their initiation commitments, with the sacred within nature and with themselves, and generally fill themselves with the connection to 'all there is'.

They have a whole repertoire of means and tools with which to do this. Nature awareness walks, meditation exercises, deep listening and merging with forces in nature, nature initiations such as the burial of the warrior, wilderness camps and pilgrimages to sacred sites are all part of it. Connecting with the spirit essences that underlie nature's manifest forms, such as plants, trees, mountains, rocks, water, stars and planets, is vital. Vision quests take place in nature, where the most profound, transformational experiences can be had, especially when experienced facilitators conduct the quests in a wild environment. Much ceremonial and ritualistic work takes place outside, often around fires, including the sweat lodge, medicine wheel, seasonal, moon and medicine plant ceremonies.

I have facilitated many groups that included work in nature. The transformation in people is astonishing, especially if the work includes vision quests or drumming, dancing and nature ceremonies around fires: the masks fall away, the enjoyment of mental, emotional and physical freedom becomes tangible, creative expression soars and heartfelt connections grow.

Reconnect with the sacred in nature and your own nature

I have already introduced you to working with the four nature directions of the wheel (*in the previous chapter*) and suggested that you do rituals and ceremonies outside (*in Chapter 8*). Here I will give you some ideas on how you can work by yourself to connect with the sacred in nature and your own sacred nature, nourish your soul and increase your emotional and mental wellbeing.

Become conscious of the gifts of nature

An easy yet essential shamanic practice is to become more conscious of nature's life-giving and life-sustaining forces and developing gratitude and appreciation.

Remember that every breath we take, every drop of water we drink and most of the foods we eat comes from nature. The joy we feel when the rays of the sun touch us, the refreshing coolness of the wind on our skin, the sound of a river that calms us – these blessings and so many more are nature's gifts.

If you want to go a step further, remind yourself that the meat you eat comes from an animal and the fruit you enjoy comes from a plant or tree, and thank their spirits. You can also bless the food you eat, give thanks for it and begin to leave little offerings outside for the spirits of nature.

Be seen by Mother Nature

A powerful and moving way to connect with nature is to be seen by Mother Nature. We have a tendency to look at our environment and forget that we are also being looked at.

Exercise: Being seen by Mother Nature

I often use this exercise and have also used it with clients and groups. For most people, the experience feels loving and nurturing. It provides a delightful way to experience being part of something bigger that loves you. It is also very healing, especially at emotionally demanding times in your life. Do it as often as you can and the positive, loving regard of nature will work its magic on your psyche.

- Taking a notepad, find a quiet spot outside.
- Spend some time stilling yourself: breathe deeply, rattle or drum.
- Close your eyes and imagine that you are being seen by nature. Or ask to be seen. Ask Mother Nature to look at you as one of her children, with love.
- Be aware of feelings, thoughts, images, sensations, intuitions and sounds.
- Open your eyes when you feel the urge to do so. Write down what you have experienced.

Honour the spirit of place and your own place

Before beginning work in a place, all the shamanic teachers I have met have honoured its spirit. During the honouring they get to know the spirit of the place and often they are given signs about it, its energy and what is required to work beneficially within it.

When working in a centre in Cornwall, I greeted the spirits of the place and was instructed to climb a nearby hill, greet the guardian of the stone circle there and ask his permission to work within the circle. I hadn't planned to do any work in the circle, but after greeting the guardian, I decided to conduct a ceremony there as the space felt very powerful. Needless to say, it turned out to be one of the most profound ceremonies I have ever facilitated.

Another time, when I walked around the grounds of a camp greeting the spirits, I met a deer. She was young and small and stood there looking at me for quite a while. I changed part of the programme to include more gentle and feminine aspects, which turned out to be exactly what the group needed.

The spirit of a place consists of many layers and ingredients, including all the human imprints. But in this chapter, as we are connecting with nature, we will use the indigenous definition of spirit and spirituality of 'place', which is based on the ecology of a place: every landscape or place is a web and together they form the great web of Being and Becoming. So it is the spirit of this smaller web within the large web of life that you want to get to know and honour.

Exercise: Honouring the spirit of a place

- Go to a place in nature.
- Still yourself: rattle, drum, breathe.
- Close your eyes. Ask the spirit of the place to connect with you or call it with a drum or rattle.
- Listen and be aware: you will get hunches, images, maybe words, a sudden knowing, a feeling.
- When you feel that you are connected, ask the spirit of the place any question you choose and note the answer.
- Leave something to honour the spirit or conduct a little ceremony.

Connect with the spirit of your own place

If you are in harmony with the spirit of your own place, you will find that your life runs more smoothly and that the place you live in will support you. When you are doing it for the first time, it is beneficial to journey to the spirit of your own place. Later, you can just briefly tune into it whenever necessary.

Exercise: Journey to meet the spirit of your own place

(For the structure of a shamanic journey, see page 63.)

Your intent is:

> *'I am journeying to meet the spirit of this place and ask them to advise me how to best be in this place and serve it so that it also serves me.'*

- Let the journey unfold.
- Write it down afterwards.

This is an exercise I really would advise you to do, because it's astonishing how much information you receive when you contact the spirit of your own place. You will be shown which adjustments to make or which energies are strong and which need strengthening or clearing. You can also 'feed' the place by leaving offerings or create a ceremony to thank and honour it. It is helpful to tune into the spirit of your place repeatedly.

Connect with the spiritual aspects of all living things

In shamanism we connect with and get to know the spirit aspects – the essences – of living things in nature, which also helps us to strengthen our own spiritual aspect. I would advise you to connect with the spirit aspects of trees, plants, rocks, mountains, forests and rivers, or of the elements, such as water, earth, fire and air. Of course you can't do this all at once, but you can begin. There are many ways to do this.

Exercise: Connecting outside

- Go outside. Find a spot that feels right or go to the tree, plant, river or whatever you want to connect with.
- Call in spirit.
- Go into a meditative trance: breathe, rattle, drum or sing and close your eyes.
- Tell the tree (plant, rock, etc.) that you would like to connect.
- Imagine that you are connecting in whatever form feels right to you.
- Be patient. Listen deeply. Just stay connected and become aware of images, hunches, sounds, feelings and sudden insights.
- You will know when you have finished for the time being. Thank the tree and write down what you remember.

Exercise: Connecting via the shamanic journey

Another way to connect is through the shamanic journey. Your intent will be:

> *'I am journeying to the middle world to connect with the essence of this tree. I ask the tree to teach me.'*

Then let the journey unfold.

Nature walks: enhance your awareness and connect

Conscious walks are a pleasant way to enhance your awareness of nature and your connection to it. If you live in an urban area, go to a park. If you have access to countryside, walk anywhere that feels right to you.

Exercise: A connecting awareness walk

This is a nice way to practise receiving the 'whispers of the sacred in nature'. You can do this in four stages:

- Formulate an intent, such as 'I am connecting with the sacred in nature', and repeat it a few times as you walk.
- Listen for a few minutes, then sense and feel.
- Next, become aware of plants, trees and wildlife.
- Fourthly, connect to the ground. Sense your connection with the Earth.

You don't have to do anything else. The exercise itself produces the connection.

Exercise: 'Let something find you' walk

This awareness walk will connect you with spirits.

- Walk consciously and silently in a relaxed manner.
- After a few minutes, state an intent along the lines of:

  'I ask for whatever wants to find me to find me.'

- After stating your intent a few times, just keep walking with awareness. Be assured something will find you. It usually comes in a surprising form, is needed in your life and captures your attention.

During practice in a group, people were found by a variety of things. One participant was found by her voice. She started singing and loved it. Needless to say, she was a very quiet person, who rarely said anything.

Another was found by a buzzard, which he watched spellbound as it circled in the sky above its prey. Whilst watching, he received the timely message that he needed to bring more focus into his life.

Another was found by her freedom and courage. She vividly remembered a time in her childhood when she often cycled in the village and nearby woods with friends. She recalled the excitement, the feeling of freedom and, most importantly, her own courage.

Yet another person was found by silence, which she saw as a gift. She suddenly became aware that she had walked for a long time without her usual intensely present 'mind-chatter'.

There are many ways of creating 'awareness walks'. You can even do these exercises just sitting still in nature. The important thing is that you focus on nature, not your inner state. This will create a resonating inner state, which makes the connection.

Part III
THE WIDER WEB OF LIFE

'The eyes of the future are looking down on us and they are praying for us to see beyond our own time.'

Terry Tempest Williams, *Refuge*

Chapter 12

Embedded in the Cycle of Life

In shamanism all life is seen as eternal in the sense that it exists in the underlying fields, the spirit worlds. This doesn't mean that all strands of shamanism believe in reincarnation, but it does mean that everything exists in one way or another in spirit form in the 'pool of consciousness' and returns to it after the body dies. Without going into a philosophical discussion here, I want to share with you some practical ways of experiencing this whilst addressing three important strands within the shamanic cosmology: creation myths, the connection to ancestral spirits and the subject of death and dying.

Creation stories: the power of formation myths

Every culture creates its own significant myths which shape its basic world-views and beliefs. Myths create and reflect our views of who we are and our standing within the whole of creation. They also describe and transmit, in all spiritual traditions and all religions, the mysterious and magical. Myths work with archetypes and activate the parts of our brain that are receptive to archetypal material, through which we understand and process the timeless concepts of the forces at work within creation generally and humanity specifically. It is this understanding, on levels beyond our conscious awareness, that shapes much of our walk upon this Earth. Therefore such stories are great teachers, but also influence us subconsciously, positively or negatively, in ways beyond our control.[1]

Creation myths especially form the foundations of our views of the world, our place within creation and what life is all about. Contemporary religious ones influence our societies greatly, whether we are conscious of it or not. For example, the creation story in Judaism, Christianity and Islam is hierarchical, with a creator at the top. Humans are the 'crown of creation', made in his image, and with, according to Genesis, the right to subdue the Earth and to rule over all other creatures. In this view, not only is humanity superior to – and separate from – the rest of creation, but the masculine is also superior to the feminine. Eve, created from Adam's rib, is by definition second in the human hierarchy and worth less. She is furthermore portrayed as the one who ate first from the forbidden fruit of knowledge and gave it to Adam, so, in some texts, is responsible for humanity's banishment from paradise. This has laid the basis for the current widespread detrimental attitude towards the feminine.

Creation stories in Earth-based traditions and systems are quite different. What strikes us most is the inclusion of animal spirits as vital forces, the understanding that it takes the feminine and the masculine in equal measures to create a whole, the depiction of the Earth as the mother and the fact that the laws laid down within the myths support an interconnected view of all life on Earth.

Expand your sense of self: find your own creation myth

We each have a personal creation story that is very deeply rooted in our unconscious mind. This will reflect the creation myth of the dominant religion in our society and our society's beliefs about what human life is and what we are here for.

My first experience of exploring the story of creation – and my own creation – showed me how much such unconsciously held stories restrict our sense of who we are:[2]

> *In the beginning, if there was a beginning at all, there was the joy of pure consciousness. Pure consciousness was JOY, because this was the only way it knew how to BE.*
>
> *Consciousness was sending out, quite involuntarily, sparks of joy as it danced its own way of Being. And as pure consciousness has danced since eternity – and still dances now – it sent out countless sparks. Some sparks travelled faster and faster, in all directions. Some travelled together, some separately. Some ran out of steam after some time and some were so strong that they are still travelling now. But no matter where they are, they are everywhere, invisible to the eye, filling a space that has no boundaries.*
>
> *Some sparks joined together and formed planets, stars and galaxies. Many sparks formed the sun. Their overwhelming joyful dances created heat and warmth and light for the Earth, helping to give birth to life as we know it on our planet.*
>
> *I am one of the sparks that came from the sun. I*

am fire and light and warmth. When I entered the atmosphere of Earth, I connected with water and what we know as air, and so I became the rainbow. My task on this Earth is to be the rainbow, coming out of the pure light spark that I am. The rainbow is a bridge. It shines in many colours and it needs all the elements to be visible, but it is pure white light beyond its visible manifestation.

And, just to add, everything is created in the same way: out of the sparks of pure consciousness that was in the beginning, if there was a beginning, and will be at the end, if there is an end.

How to find your own creation story

You will find that if you are asked about yourself, the story you will typically tell starts at birth and ends with death. But once you are able to enlarge the context of your story, your view of yourself and your world widens and becomes enriched.

The best way to find your own mind-broadening creation story is via a shamanic journey to the upper world. You need to be conscientious in setting it up and not be tempted to use a shortcut. This is a profound journey. You will be astonished how much it will widen your perspective of who you are and what you are here for.

Exercise: Finding your own creation story

- Journey to the upper world. Your intent is:

'I am journeying to the upper world to learn about creation and my own creation, and about my task on this Earth. I ask all my guides, teachers and ancestral spirits to help me.'

- Immediately after finishing your journey, write your creation story, as I did in my story above. It should be a story, not a transcript of the journey. This is quite important, because as you write it the story will unfold further and will bring itself into form.

Integrating your creation story into your life

My own creation story tells me what I am. The rainbow is important to me, because I have many facets and for some time I tortured myself with the idea that I should specialize in something. This has long passed, because I now understand that some people are excellent at focusing on one thing only, whilst others feel restricted if they cannot express different parts of themselves. I also understand that I am indeed a bridge. I see myself as forming a bridge between the contemporary psychological and therapeutic world and the ancient shamanic psycho-spiritual one.

So, once you have your own creation story, embody it. Dance it, paint it, create something that reminds you of it and put it on your altar. Find a symbol of your bigger story and put it in places that are important. For example, I have a rainbow painted inside my drum frame. Nobody sees it but me. It reminds me of who I am, especially when I try to narrow myself down to please others. Most importantly, use your creation myth to help you to express yourself, to understand that you are more than your story of this life and that you have purpose.

Widen your circle: connect with ancestors and descendants

An African shaman said once to me, 'You people are very poor and alone. You have deadened the magical within and you don't even have a connection to your ancestors.' This West African healer, from a small tribal community in one of the poorest nations in the world, echoed the opinion of many shamans who believe that we live one-dimensional, spiritually poor lives because we have disconnected from the mystical and our spirit ancestors. Indigenous cultures see this loss of connection to our ancestors as a highly detrimental development: it turns us into individuals without roots, leaves us without direct access to the wisdom of our ancestral spirits and contributes to the disrespect of the old in modern societies. Critically, it adds to losing sight of the generations that will come after us.

On a soul level, we are connected to our ancestors, whether we are aware of it or not, and once we begin to value that connection, we begin to feel more rooted and develop a sense of belonging to a wider community.

In a traditional sense, ancestors are all the people who have lived before us. Close ancestors are those who are connected to us via bloodline, place and soul group. Place is important because indigenous communities don't move much, so the ancestors who are connected to us via place have knowing about the place and its underlying spirit forces. A soul group is a group of people we have been connected to on our soul journey over many lifetimes. To put it simply, they have been on a similar journey to us. If we meet somebody from our soul group, we will automatically feel we have a bond with them, even if we don't quite know why. We are more energetically connected to ancestors of the same soul group, so we can reach them more easily when seeking advice and support. All these ancestors form a network that we could call our wider ancestral circle.

It is the ancestors' responsibility to hold the memories and wisdom gained from the beginning of humankind. It is the responsibility of the living to learn from them – their wisdom and their mistakes – and so to change and evolve.[3] It is in this sense that indigenous cultures are in frequent contact with their ancestors, revere them, use them as role models, connect with them as helping spirits and learn from them.

Connecting to spirit ancestors

I work with ancestral spirits and have used ancestral connection exercises in groups and with individual clients, always beneficially. We all can connect to ancestral spirits who have wisdom and want to help, guide and protect us. It is worth mentioning in this context that for many people, the ancestors who carry the most wisdom and can act as role models are often not recent ones, but lived way back in time.[4]

One of my ancestral spirit guides, who came to me during a vision quest, is of mixed race, Native American and Caucasian. She is old and very wise in the sense that she went through much suffering and also knows the old and the new ways. I honour her and I ask her for advice, and she often just shows up, especially when I facilitate drumming groups or ceremonies.

Exercise: Journey to connect with an ancestral guide

Your intent is:

> *'I am going to journey to the upper world to meet an ancestral spirit who means well by me and can help me on life's journey.'*

- Get to know your spirit ancestor. Ask questions. Be with them. Learn, get advice, talk to them. They are usually very communicative.
- Come back when you hear the call-up beat.

Your ancestor spirit will often turn into a guide and teacher for you if you keep in contact with them. Or they may already be a guide and teacher, but you haven't identified them as an ancestor. My partner was aware of a guide called 'Nana' who sometimes came to him in dreams. It took a few years before he realized that this was his grandmother, who had died before he was born.

Integrating and working with your ancestral connections

Contact your ancestor spirits whenever you feel the need. They are close by and easy to envisage and communicate with once you have made the first contact through a journey. Craft something that has the qualities of your ancestor guide or paint a picture or write it down. Honour your ancestors by putting something on the altar that represents them – after all, you owe them your life. Attempt an ancestor ceremony, such as the tree ceremony (*see page 97*) or a fire ceremony (see *page 96*), sending your gratitude up to the spirit world through the smoke.

Include 'helping ancestral spirit' in your spirit calling before ceremonies or journeys.

Connecting to descendants

Another aspect of an energetic cosmology is that the underlying fields not only hold all consciousness to date but also all potentialities of the future. In other words, all our dreaming, thoughts, actions and more influence this field and change the future. This means that we have a duty to take future generations into account, not only by leaving an Earth that can be inhabited, but also leaving them systems and values that ensure good, balanced ways of living. Oren Lyons' famous statement 'What about the seventh generation? Where are you taking them? What will they have?'[5] describes the questions we, who rarely think further than one or two generations ahead, need to ask ourselves.

Part of shamanic work is to develop a stronger connection with future generations, not theoretically, but by experiencing the connection and beginning to take those who will come after us into account in the way we live now. I have found that the best way to begin is to journey to the future to meet a descendant, somebody who hasn't been born yet. This could theoretically be anybody, but it is usually somebody who is close to you energetically either through bloodline, place or soul group.

Exercise: Journey to connect with a descendant

Your intent is:

'I am going to journey forward in time to meet one of my

descendants and find out what I can do now to make their lives better.'

- With power animals and guides present, let the journey unfold, observing the life of one of your descendants.
- Listen carefully to what they say. Promise before you come back that you will follow their advice and take them into account.
- Come back when you hear the call-up beat.

It is not surprising that the majority of journeys to descendants lead people to rather alarming places that are often sterile, barren, poor and sometimes undercover because the natural environment isn't habitable any longer. Most of us have an understanding that we need to change our ways, but we often don't quite know how. It is therefore important to include 'and find out what I can do now to make their lives better' in the intent. In groups I have found that every participant finds at least one concrete way to contribute to a better life for their distant descendants.

Integration work with your descendants

Whatever the outcome of your journey to your descendants, implement it. You can also create something to represent your descendants on your altar. You can remind yourself that there will be people coming after you and include them in your blessings. I often tune into my descendants before I make decisions, especially when they influence the generations to come, asking if the choice I am about to make will benefit or harm them.

Shamanism helps us in many ways to develop an expanded consciousness. Connecting to our ancestors and descendants is one of them. Whilst giving us more roots, it takes us away from our self-centred ways and embeds us consciously into the wider field of our family lines and networks, turning us into conscious co-creators of a positive future.

Death as part of life: the gifts we receive when facing death

Life and death together create what we perceive in a spiritual sense as the whole of life. Every spiritual approach pays attention to death, trying to understand what happens when - and after - the body dies. We cannot talk about the cycle of life - and about shamanism - without addressing these questions. The shaman faces death, embraces it and learns from it.

Unfortunately, the more we separate from the rest of creation, the more we advance scientifically and medically and the more we subscribe to a materialistic world-view, the more we seem to deny and fear death. Fear of dying has, of course, a rightful place in human life. After all, we possess a strong inbuilt survival instinct. The problem lies in our increasing need to avoid the subject of death whilst spending incredible amounts of material resources and personal energy on 'staying young'. When, despite all our efforts, we still have to face old age and dying, we even spend vast resources on keeping ourselves artificially alive.

This disowning of ageing and dying, which are part of the natural cycle of all manifest life, keeps us stuck in a restricted body consciousness. It denies us the gifts we receive when we consciously face the fact that we have only a limited time in this body, especially the gifts of developing soul and spirit awareness and expanding our consciousness.

The gifts we receive

I have faced death in various ways. Each experience brought the gift of learning. My first conscious experience of death, which made a lasting impression, happened when I was very young. Looking into the eyes of a dying rabbit, I realized that we were equal on one level: we both wanted to live and we both would die. I learned that death was a great equalizer and this early understanding led to the conviction that all life was indeed precious.

Later, at the House of the Dying in Calcutta, I learned that a 'good and dignified death' was vitally important. 'Good and dignified' means, in shamanic terms, to be prepared and ready, with people around us who are catering for our soul's departure in surroundings that are beneficial to leaving this body. This idea of a good death became even more poignant to me when I worked in northern Uganda as a trauma specialist and was confronted with the indescribable horrors of war and its cruel and traumatic ways of dying.

When my parents died - my father in a dignified way, almost as if he had decided that it was his time, my mother after a heartbreaking period of deterioration, neither ready nor prepared - I began to ask myself whether the fear of death had to be faced.

In my twenties in an ashram in India, I had a frightening dismemberment vision which brought me to the brink of death - or at least that's how it felt - and much later I went through a near-death experience when my heart failed. Although I survived both, they resulted in the death of parts of my 'I' as I knew it and in the knowing that there are realities outside our consensus one.

That life is eternal, not necessarily in human form but in a realm of consciousness beyond it, was confirmed to me after participating in shamanic initiations and medicine plant ceremonies. I also know that Bill Plotkin is right when he states, 'You are unlikely to uncover and embody your soul if you are living as if your ego and body are immortal.'[6]

My own experiences, frightening as some of them were, have given me many gifts. Facing our own mortality is not easy, but it brings to the fore what really matters, forces us to focus and leads us to strive to lead a worthwhile life whilst realizing that life in this body is indeed brief and precious. In this sense, death is a great teacher. My life certainly became more focused as a result of my experiences. I am also more compassionate now, with myself and others. I am more courageous and fear less. I base my choices increasingly on what is meaningful and purposeful, what expands my consciousness and what nourishes my heart and soul, whilst striving for authenticity in the process. Disturbing as the heart failure was, it produced a focused space within which gave me the opportunity to look again at my life and decide what I wanted to let go. I resigned as the course director of a therapy institute, took on less work as a psychologist and focused almost completely on my own spiritual growth and on the shamanic side of my work, which resulted in my first book as well as much writing and teaching about it.

Most importantly though, when we face death, we get to know our soul in the process and we give ourselves the gift of peace, which comes with accepting the cycle of all manifest life, and – so I hope – the gift of dying more whole.

Working with death in shamanism

Facing death is the most important initiation rite that a traditional shaman goes through, sometimes repeatedly. These initiations are not always controlled in the sense that they are part of an initiatory path with a teacher being present. Many shamanic callings come about via severe physical illnesses, trauma experiences and what we now call 'spiritual emergencies'.

Traditionally, these experiences serve a few vital purposes:

- Death becomes a teacher of the cycles of all life and is consulted as a teacher, including on how to live in the 'right way' and die a 'good death'.
- Such experiences throw the initiate into spirit realms and intense encounters with spirits who need to be explored and connected with. Some of them, such as the spirits of the underworlds, need to be struggled and fought with and overcome. In the process the shaman gains strength and knowledge, and their old self dies. They are reborn back into the body, transformed from a 'wounded healer' into a powerful shaman and bringing with them the knowledge and knowing of the other worlds.
- The shaman will, through the experience of dying and being reborn, learn how to overcome their survival

> instinct, a mastery that allows them to access and traverse the spirit worlds via out-of-body flights and also to learn about the soul's journey into such worlds after death, which is knowledge required in their work as a psychopomp.[7]

Most traditional shamans, having been through death and rebirth initiations, would state that they are 'already dead' and therefore don't fear death because their experiences have transformed them profoundly. They now know that they are in essence spirit and that death is just another form of reality. The time of death is seen as a transition stage between lives, as the spirit essence, light soul or consciousness leaves the body and lives on in another dimension, in spirit, with the ancestors.

Initiation rituals for contemporary seekers

In contemporary shamanism there are many ways of working with death. I am not suggesting that you try them at home, so I won't describe them in depth, just give you some information.

Initiation rites in contemporary shamanism are not frequent and rarely as profound as the ones in traditional shamanism. For most contemporary shamanic practitioners, the journey is an unfolding process that leads deeper into shamanism, with parts of the practitioner dying and others being born in the process.

Having said that, there are rites and ceremonies that include facing death, though we often have to travel to indigenous teachers to participate in them. An initiation ritual in which I participated was held in Ecuador in a sulphur cave. The build-up to it was, for me, more nerve-racking than the actual experience, as we were repeatedly told that we could literally die in that cave if our intent and connection to spirit weren't impeccable. Not giving into fears and overcoming my survival instinct – by staying in the cave much longer than was comfortable – were the major outcomes for me.[8]

Another intense ceremonial rite I participated in was the 'burial of the warrior', led by Victor Sanchez, a shamanic practitioner from the Toltec tradition in Mexico. The main focus of the ritual comes when you spend the night in a grave, covered with earth, with only a small breathing hole, the size of a tennis ball, ensuring a supply of oxygen. The burial is mainly about facing your fears and overcoming them and about renewal through spending a night deep in Mother Earth and emerging into the light at sunrise. For me this was a 'facing the fear of death' experience, as spending a night completely covered in a dark space brought to the fore an intense fear of suffocating. It offered me a chance to trust my spirit helpers and to alleviate many fears during the preparation phase, which is done with the help of an obsidian mirror. I loved the emerging phase, experiencing utter bliss and a renewed feeling of 'coming from the sun' as I came back out into the light.

There are also more profound trainings and apprenticeships in Africa or South America which include strong rites, the repeated ingestion of medicine plants and deep dreaming practices that focus on death and rebirth (*see also chapters 13 and 14*).

Generally speaking, everything that includes death and

rebirth rites should only be attempted with an experienced shamanic teacher. Nevertheless, you can make a start by exploring the subject.

How you can start by yourself

Journeys and movement are nice ways to start working with the transition of the soul from the body to the other worlds. As with all profound journeys, these work best if you set them up ceremonially and really take your time.

Exercise: Journey to explore the realm after death

A good way to start is to journey to be shown the realm to which you will go when you die.

Intent:

> *'I am going to journey to be shown the realm I will go to when I die. I ask for help from spirit guides and teachers.'*

Let the journey unfold. Your spirit guides and helpers will accompany you on this journey. Often others will show up spontaneously and you might also meet loved ones who are already in the spirit world. The realm you will reach is beautiful.

Exercise: Journey to become familiar with your own physical death

This journey takes you to the point where your spirit is leaving the body and you are arriving in Bardo, the place between the worlds. You will be in spirit form and this dissociated state guarantees that physical and emotional reactions are kept to a minimum.

Intent:

> *'I am going to journey to observe my own death, the moment my soul leaves my body. I will be in spirit form and ask my spirit allies to be with me.'*

Let the journey unfold. A good learning when you journey in this way is that the moment the spirit leaves the body, death really does lose its sting and is experienced as something quite natural and sometimes astonishingly beautiful.

Dancing your last dance

As you may be aware, I personally love all dancing practices within shamanism. So I have to say that a great way to work with death is to dance your last journey, your transition journey between this world and the other. This should be done repeatedly.

Exercise: Dancing your last journey

To dance your last journey, set up the space, call in spirit and your spirit helpers and repeat your intent as you would do on any other journey, but instead of travelling in your imagination, just dance! You can use the drumming download or any powerful rhythmic music.

During the dance you might encounter memories, a range of emotions and the people you love. Specific totem animals or guides connected to death and dying might show up, as might significant people who have already left this body.

Much healing can be done within the dance and much love is always present. You express whatever you experience until you are peaceful and ready to let go. Then you dance your spirit leaving your body, which is always a very joyful experience.

The dance journey lasts as long as it takes.

I have danced this dance a few times and have often had a jaguar present – the power of the underworld. It shows up when I am fearful, but in the end retreats lovingly and kind of pleased and is replaced by light energy and bliss.

Does all this talk about death sound dark and gloomy to you? Let me assure you it is not. Work with death, rebirth and initiation rites is not advised at the beginning of your shamanic path, but when done within a shamanic set-up and with the right facilitator, it is amazingly freeing. It deals with a reality for which most of us are completely unprepared. It puts things into perspective, heals many wounds, gives us insight into what happens when the soul leaves, and, according to shamanic teachings, gives us some control over the way we die, as the way we envisage it, the way we think about it and the way we desire it to occur influences how our death will manifest.

Chapter 13

Sacred Medicine Plants

Psychoactive plants are perceived as great teachers in indigenous cultures all over the world: gifts from the plant kingdom and plant spirits to help us heal, expand our consciousness and connect with and work within the spirit worlds. Indigenous shamans have therefore developed a profound body of knowledge about them, including their physical, mental and psychological effects and how to set up plant journeys and ceremonies beneficially.

Strong visionary states such as those brought about by sacred plant teachers break down cognitive barriers and ego defences and open neural gateways usually closed to us, thus enabling us to experience worlds we didn't know existed. In shamanism, entheogens are not, however, used for recreational purposes and should not be taken because we want to have a spiritual adventure. They can be part of the shamanic journey to expand consciousness, connect, heal and become whole, but they are neither 'quick fixes' nor can they replace the psycho-spiritual journey itself. The ingestion of plant medicines can elicit floods of sheer fear and terror as well as awe, bliss, ecstasy, all-encompassing connectedness and overwhelming love. Whatever we experience will have transformational effects and change our view of the world.

Traditional plant ceremonies

Traditionally, psychoactive plants are always taken in a respectful way that honours the teaching spirit of the plant. They are ingested after a period of preparation, with clear intent and in a ceremonial setting, with spirit forces invited and present. The taking of the plant medicines is usually accompanied by the shaman singing or chanting and/or the use of drums and rattles. The combination of all these ingredients is seen as essential when journeying into the various worlds with a specific intent, to receive teachings and visions, to cure illnesses of a mental, physical, spiritual or emotional nature, for divination and prophecy or to connect with spirits and guides and with the divine.

Plant ceremonies usually take place in darkness, sometimes around a fire, outside or within a lodge, and will last all night. Often plants are taken during consecutive nights, with the doses being increased each time.

Every traditional shaman who works with teacher plants has to go through a lengthy training and initiation into plant medicine before working with other people. Traditional shamans either journey alone or with the tribe sitting in a circle around them, and in some tribes everybody participates. Now, as more and more seekers from all over the world are partaking, and as plant ceremonies are increasingly becoming part of contemporary shamanism, they generally take the form of group retreats, with all participants taking the psychoactive substances on consecutive nights.

Participants in plant journeys will have individual experiences and the experienced shaman, *ayahuasquero* or *huachamera* will be connected to, influence and guide whatever is going on for each person and show remarkable insight into the worlds and visions people encounter during their specific journey.

Plant medicine works in various ways. I have taken part in mushroom ceremonies and through my experiences and visions have come to understand much about the underlying worlds, but also about the dark shadow-sides and wounding of my psyche and the shadows of the world.

Some people, especially those who have experienced great mental and emotional suffering in their lives or have suppressed much shadow material, will go through experiences that can be quite frightening whilst clearing out mental and emotional patterns held within the mind, body and energy body. The visions encountered can also be of a violent and frightening nature, and some plant mixtures, such as ayahuasca, often produce vomiting during the purification phase.

But even if some people go through frightening phases during the experience, the outcome will be positive, as plant teacher will always give us what we need and we will end up in worlds that are beautiful and gain much healing and insight in the process.

A friend of mine, the amazing shamanic writer and teacher Matthew Pallamary, gives a good general description of how teacher plants speak to us when we ingest them:

> *...they speak through colors, patterns, abstractions, and archetypes, introducing concepts beyond limited rational thinking. Moreover, the language of teacher plants unfolds their cosmic wisdom, blossoming in geometric permutations that speak in mathematical progressions using the universal language of sacred geometry to reveal the true nature of the divine unfolding of conscious intelligence that permeates all that is.*[1]

Nothing will prepare you for the experience, as so much depends on the plant teacher, the shaman, the spirits and your mental/emotional state at the time of participating, but let me assure you, a well-conducted medicine plant ceremony will 'blow your mind' in a consciousness-enhancing sense. I can therefore not stress enough that it is important to have experienced shamans/leaders present who have a sound knowledge of the workings of the specific plant spirits, their physical and mental effects and the visions that can be encountered, and who can judge the strength of the doses given.

It is interesting that patterns of ceremonial usage of psychoactive plants are almost identical in different cultures around the world:

- The role of an experienced shaman/guide is vital, as their knowing, preparation, intent, guidance, singing, chanting and use of drums or other instruments shape the quality and content of the experience.

- Strong visions, beautiful as well as frightening, are often encountered and intuitive knowing – and much knowledge – is conveyed by the plant teacher.
- The boundaries between 'this reality' and 'the spirit worlds' can be crossed. People see these other realities or journey energetically to them, or both.
- Spirit entities such as the spirits of animals, trees, plants, guides and ancestors present themselves in intense ways and seem very real. In some cases, people shapeshift into one or more of them. The spirits can also become allies and helpers.
- Healing experiences can be very profound and also emotionally challenging. Very profound plant journeys can involve dismemberment, restructuring and rebirthing experiences as well as the reintegration of split-off soul parts and milder experiences of physical and psychological healing.[2]

The sacred plants: ibogaine, San Pedro, peyote, mushrooms and ayahuasca

Here is a brief overview of the plant medicines that are now being increasingly taken by seekers from and in non-indigenous societies.

Ibogaine

Iboga is an African rainforest shrub containing, in its root bark, the psychedelic alkaloid ibogaine, which has been used by African shamans for thousands of years for spiritual development and rites of passage. Ancestral spirits are generally prominent in African ceremonies. Iboga ceremonies usually last for 24 hours, with the ancestral spirits, drums, chants and rhythms working together with the plant to 'break open the head'.

Ibogaine is now also used as an effective addiction interrupter for many substances, including heroin, methadone, methamphetamine, cocaine, alcohol and nicotine. It can induce intense reprocessing and a complete rebirth experience, it alleviates physical withdrawal symptoms and it seems that the plant knows what people need to experience or re-experience – and process – in order to overcome substance addiction and heal.[3]

San Pedro

San Pedro is a cactus growing in the Andes. Its active ingredient is mescaline. Set up and prepared ceremonially, it is consumed in groups, often around a fire, with altars being built to represent the dark and light spirits that can be encountered.

Lesley Myburgh, who runs shamanic retreats and has led ceremonies with San Pedro for a long time, describes the effects of the sacred cactus:

> *It is a master teacher... It helps us to heal, to grow, to learn and awaken, and assists us in reaching higher states of consciousness. I have been very blessed to have experienced many miracles: people being cured of all sorts of illnesses just by drinking this sacred plant. We use it to reconnect to the Earth and to realize that there is no separation between you, me, the Earth and the Sky. We are all One. It's one thing to read that, but to actually experience this oneness is the most beautiful gift we can receive.*[4]

Peyote

Peyote is a Mexican cactus. The sacred plant teacher of the Huichol, the Cora and Tarahumara, it now also has a big following in North America. The active ingredient is, again, mescaline.

After extensive preparation, the Huichol undertake a yearly traditional pilgrimage, called the peyote hunt, to the sacred site of Wirikuta (Paradise), where the cactus can be found. It is a symbolic return to their origins, to where 'their mother lives', in order to 'find their life'. Dances, fasting, prayers, storytelling, purification and much weeping accompany the ceremonial intake of peyote, with the shaman performing healing. Peyote is also taken back to the community, sold to other tribes and used in between pilgrimages.

I took mescaline a long time ago. It struck me as a gentle, rather mild teacher, being energizing and bringing soft visions and vibrations, rather beautiful emotional states and experiences of connection and joy.

Mushrooms

First brought to the attention of the Western world by Gordon Wasson[5] and popularized by the writings of Carlos Castaneda, mushrooms were amongst the first psychedelics sought by spiritual seekers from all over the world. They can be found in many parts of the globe, but the best-known traditional mushroom ceremonies take place in Mexico. During these, the shaman chants and sings songs throughout the night, weaving a web of the elements and spirit.

From my experience, lower doses of mushrooms increase visual perception, allowing underlying fields, energetic movement and vibrant colours to be seen, whilst high doses induce full visionary experiences. I want to describe one of my own here:

> *Suddenly, the world is alive. Everything moves gently: the trees, the mountains, the plants and the ground. The air around me shows whirling patterns in pastel colours. Fascinated, I observe my perception changing, whilst the movement of everything holds me spellbound. The sudden and undoubted insight that everything is alive sends me into an ecstatic state of bliss – until I take some more and the vision abruptly changes: I am no longer the observer, but an integral part of the experience. I seem to have been thrown out of my body and am flying through space. The speed is breathtaking. The suddenness of the event produces panic: I can feel my heart racing. I fly down a dark tunnel, where luminous eyes stare threateningly at me. I have the impression that I will hit the ground, breaking into pieces. Terror engulfs my very being. A part of me is aware of my shaking body, my beating heart and, very vaguely, of place, people and soft chanting, but I am nevertheless out of control, in a frightening place, with more and more eyes coming towards me out of the darkness.*
>
> *I don't remember all of this part of the journey, but I remember vividly the moment of knowing what to do. Whilst realizing that I have to stop trying to control this, I know I have to shapeshift into a cat, so that I can see in the dark and land softly. I begin to imitate the*

movements of a big cat, and, imagining the features of a cheetah I once observed in Africa, I am suddenly a big cat, at the bottom of a large dark space, moving safely on the ground. Ah, this is how it feels to be an animal! I love it. I stay in the form of a cat for quite a long time – or so it seems.

The next moment I remember is hearing the chanting again and feeling myself being pulled, as if through a vortex, up into a jungle landscape. I stand there, overwhelmed by the intensity of the colours, vibrations and sounds, out of control, feeling terror of the unknown creeping up on me. But before I can give in to my resurgent fear, I become aware of myself pulsating. The whole place pulsates as well – it is alive, but not threatening. My pulsating merges with that of the place and I am again in a state of utter bliss. Everything alive, me alive ... I am indeed part of this web of sheer ecstatic, vibrating, beautiful aliveness.

Ayahuasca

Ayahuasca, the 'spirit vine', 'vine of death' or 'vine of the soul', is a powerful mixture prepared by indigenous shamans in the Amazon. The leaves of the plant, which are part of the potion, contain dimethyltryptamine (DMT), a very strong hallucinogenic.

Ayahuasca ceremonies conducted by indigenous shamans and healers, mainly in Peru and Ecuador, have become extremely popular and are increasingly attended by seekers from all over the world. Well-conducted ceremonies have a dietary and energetic preparation phase; they are set up ceremonially – with spirit and intent – and take place on consecutive nights, with the doses becoming increasingly potent. Besides using rattles and sometimes drums, the shamans usually sing the *Icaros*, powerful and sacred songs through which the healing takes place and visions are encountered. For most people, ayahuasca ceremonies include a cleansing phase (*la purga*), during which they vomit.

There are many individual accounts of ayahuasca journeys.[6] I have chosen the following one because it gives powerful insights into the strong visions and emotional experiences, blissful as well as frightening, through which seekers can go:

> *Outside my physical body, the frogs, birds, insects, jaguars, and other creatures of the Peruvian Amazon fill the night air with their calls, cries, twitters and buzzes. For me there is no difference between the infinity expressing itself outside me and the infinity that I soar through inside myself. It is all one. Outside time and space, a noise from deep in the jungle sounds as if it is right beside me, startling me.*
>
> *Sometimes I feel myself fully present and aware, in two places at the same time, often in different times and dimensions.*
>
> *After experiencing the consciousness of predator and prey in the lower worlds, I have flown first as a condor, then as a hummingbird into sublime and exquisite high-frequency realities, exploding with neon luminescent pastel manifestations that defy rationality. While my*

spirit soars, my body quivers and my insides teeter on the verge of both vomiting and shitting.

I soar between agony and ecstasy as each experience awes my soul with a palette of emotions that range from heavenly bliss to a hellish, maddening terror that cannot be articulated, much less comprehended. I am vaguely aware of others sitting around me in the humid jungle night inside a circular open-air hut called a maloca. *Many of them vomit and sometimes cry out in fear or bliss as they pass through their own visions. I feel my soul connected to theirs.*

Our visions are directed by the music of a white-clad mestizo shaman who sings magical songs and plays different flutes and a stringed mandolin-like instrument called a charango. *He is the keeper of a vast body of knowledge of Amazonian healing plants that dates back to prehistoric times. His speciality is a unique combination of plants that have brought me to this visionary state that continues to unfold outside of three-dimensional reality.*

In this waking dream, where time and space become fluid, I not only soar through alien vistas of sight, sound, and feeling; I also travel through events of my life, both good and bad, often reliving them and their emotional content. Throughout my journey, I often confront hidden aspects of my Self that have been ignored and denied because of the negative emotional charge that they hold. I sometimes vomit when confronted with something particularly unpleasant, which clears it out energetically in what is called a purge.[7]

A word of caution and encouragement

As said above, plant medicine journeys should not be seen as 'quick fixes', which unfortunately we have a tendency to seek. Two more points of caution. First, there are physical health issues, such as heart conditions, high blood pressure and epilepsy, and mental health conditions, such as schizophrenia or psychosis, as well as certain forms of medication, which might be contra-indicative to partaking in psychedelic plant ceremonies. Secondly, as already indicated, you must ensure that the ceremonial shamanic leader is well trained and experienced. As offering plant ceremonies to western seekers has become a lucrative business, the market includes charlatans and pseudo-shamans.

For some people, plant medicines are part of the journey of expanding consciousness, of connection, of psycho-spiritual healing and becoming whole, but they are not the journey. The journey is an unfolding process, and if plant medicine is for you, you will know when you have reached the right point in your journey to take it. Some seekers will take it once, most will take it a few times, and for some it becomes part of the way.

The outcome for most seekers, besides personal healing and knowing, is a total change of world-view from accepting that there is only the one material world that we can experience daily with our senses to realizing that there are multiple energetic worlds and recognizing the reality of non-material spirit beings. Performed at the right time and guided by experienced shamans, medicine plant ceremonies can produce astonishing healing and transformational experiences, break through cognitive barriers and open our consciousness and our heart to the wonders of the worlds.

Chapter 14

Shamanic Work in the Dreamworld

The shaman is often also called 'the dreamer', which gives you an idea of the importance of dreaming and dream-like states within shamanism. Besides describing the dreams we have at night, there are various meanings of the word 'dreaming' or 'dream' in the context of shamanism. 'Dreaming' is sometimes used to describe everything that shamans experience and do when they alter their states and enter the spirit worlds. You might also hear the expression 'Dream of the Cosmos' or 'Dreamtime', which is based on a belief held in some cultures, such as the Aboriginal cultures of Australia, that the reality we know is the result of the Great Cosmic Dream, the Dreamtime of the ancestral souls, where the patterns of life were laid down and from which all threads of life flow. A third expression you might hear is 'the world is as you dream it', which means that the reality we experience daily with our senses is the manifest reality of the underlying individual and collective dreams, which can be experienced, explored, altered and shaped.

Here I want to focus on the dreams we have when we are asleep. These play an important role, as the consensus view in shamanism is that we access underlying layers of reality during dreaming. The dream state is a state in which the worlds meet and we all have the ability to create within them.

Dream work must therefore be seen in the context of the shaman's world-view. In shamanic tradition:

- The sleep state is a level of consciousness during which we become aware of and can enter the 'dream realm', an energetic reality. In many cultures the dreamscape – which has many layers – is seen as the underlying energetic realm of our manifest existence on this planet.
- In traditional shamanic cosmology, the shaman's flight takes them to the dream realms. Some cultures hold that it is the energy body that travels; others believe that it is the soul, or a certain energy centre, that leaves the body when we dream. However we describe the part that travels, shamanic flights into the dream worlds are not confined to the physical limitations of the body and the dreamscape is more than our personal unconscious.
- Dreams, although classified – for example into 'personal', 'prophetic', 'creation' or 'dreams with information and ancestral messages' – are generally seen as soul encounters, and dreaming, like other visionary states, is seen as connecting to the spirit worlds.

Within indigenous traditions there is much understanding of what to expect in dreams, how to deal with dream messages, how to interpret them and how to be co-creators when we dream. There are different systems in different cultures, but frequently dream work distinguishes between normal dreams, intended dreams and lucid dreams:

- Normal dreams are those we all have.
- Intended dreams are those we ask for.
- Lucid dreams are dreams where the dreamer is aware that they are dreaming. They can be intended or not.

The second distinction is between 'big dreams' and 'small dreams'. Traditionally, big dreams are dreams that concern the community or humankind as a whole, whilst 'little dreams' are for the individual. Today, we also regard some of the latter as big dreams, especially if they are dreamed repeatedly and/or if they concern major life lessons, prophecies or life directions.

There are many ways in which dreams are used in traditional and contemporary shamanism, especially, but not only, dreams that are intentional and lucid. Dreams are used, for example, for healing. In the dream state, the shaman can find information about an ailment and the healing method required and then either carry out the healing in the dream state or later in the waking state. Dreams are also seen as prophecy. If a shaman has a prophetic dream, they will act upon it without question. 'Bad' prophetic dreams may warn people about negative events so that measures, either in the dream state or in manifest reality, can be taken to avoid, redirect or rebalance them. There are also dreams that include a calling, initiation dreams that can go on over long periods of time and dreams in which spirit teaches the shaman in various ways.

Normal dreaming and sharing

Older cultures, which are aware of the different layers of reality, place much emphasis on dreaming and remembering dreams upon waking, and many tribes will share, discuss and act upon the dreams of their members regularly. Studies of several cultures, including the Shuar (Ecuador), Guarani (Brazil) and Mapuche (Chile), have found that each of the tribes considers the 'true self 'of every human being as living within their dreams. They meet in the morning in a dream circle to share, discuss and interpret their dreams, seeing a link between the messages and contents of their dreams and the way they live. Therefore they will not hesitate to make major changes based on the messages they receive in their dreams, especially if they are 'big dreams' or 'prophetic dreams'.[1] Something similar happens in Australian Aboriginal cultures: the dreams are examined collectively and the activities of the day are decided on the basis of the dreams.

Many traditions have developed vast knowledge and incredible maps of the dream worlds, such as described, for instance, in Sergio Magaña's book *The Toltec Secret*.[2] The Orang Aoli, the aboriginal people of Malaysia, are known as a 'dreaming culture', and many African tribes also put much emphasis on dreams and dreaming, seeing them as messages from their ancestors, discussing them and adjusting their lives and connections with spirit accordingly. Lee Irwin, who wrote the book *The Dream Seekers: Native American Visionary Traditions of the Great Plains*, looked at 350 dreams of 23 groups of American Indians from the Plains and found dream-sharing traditions very alive. In his view, the 'shaman's art is dramatically linked with the art of dreaming'.[3]

Intentional dreams and lucid dreams

Lucid dreaming is a state where we are 'awake' and conscious whilst we are asleep and dreaming. Although it has lately been adopted by contemporary teachers all over the world, it is in origin a shamanic skill, a method of heightened awareness in the dream, which allows shamans, healers and medicine people to access energetic powers, information, insight and help as well as the power to work within the dream state with the aim of manifestation. It is a state in which both perceptions – our normal waking awareness and our dream-state perception – begin to meet and we can therefore create within our dreams.

As with many ancient practices, we have adapted intentional lucid dreaming in a way that is more geared up to our Western desire to control and influence, although this is only part of how it is used in many shamanic cultures. In most forms of traditional shamanism (there are exceptions), lucid dreaming mainly focuses on accessing and surrendering to the forces, messages, visions and guides within the dreamscape, learning, receiving information and gaining power, and only secondly on controlling or changing the dream with the aim of manifestation. For example, the elders of the Beaver clan of the Canadian Arctic still practise 'hunting dreams' in which they ask to be shown the location of animals in their dreams before the hunters locate the game in waking life and make the kill. The elders don't dream with the intent of forcing the animals to be in a place convenient to the hunters; they use the intentional dreaming to find the place where the animals will naturally be. The same applies to the dream initiation and prophecy accounts we have from indigenous shamans such as Black

Elk. He didn't try to change anything in his lucid dreams, some of which were extremely frightening and led him to the brink of death, but accepted whatever he experienced as visions and messages from spirit.

Traditionally, lucid dreaming with intent is a skill which requires long practice and training, especially when shamanic work is undertaken within the dreamscape for the community, and 'dream shamans' or 'dream walkers' are often called to this task by spirit.

Ruby Modesto, a medicine woman of the Desert Cahuilla, received her call during dreaming. She describes the mastery of 13 levels of dreaming in her book *Not for Innocent Ears: Spiritual Traditions of a Desert Cahuilla Medicine Woman*.[4] For her, the first two levels of dreaming are quite ordinary and the 'real shamanic dreaming' begins after that. She describes how, ahead of the dreaming, she decides where she wants to go or what she wants to experience or be shown, then, whilst dreaming the first lucid dream, she plans what she wants to dream in the second dream. In the second lucid dream, she plans the third dream, and so on. She explains that it takes great skill to keep track of the levels of dreaming and describes how she was comatose in the morning at one point during her learning, because her soul, which had travelled through the different dream realms, was lost within them and she couldn't find her way back into her body.

Even on a much simpler level, lucid dreaming is acknowledged in all strands of shamanism as a very powerful tool. The contemporary Native American healer and dream walker Rolling Thunder, when interviewed by Stanley Krippner, suggested that lucid dreaming was a more reliable source of visions than mind-altering plants, provided the dreamer knew the intent and direction of the journey.[5]

In contemporary circles, lucid dreaming is used for reasons similar to those described above. The shamanic practitioner might ask for a dream to show them what is needed to heal a client; they might ask for a prophetic dream, or for insight into an issue, or to meet and be taught by specific spirits, teachers and guides. They might ask for a dream about a lost soul, which they will guide to other realms; they might use lucid dreaming for shapeshifting or prophecy or to counteract negative forces, which they will encounter in the lucid dream state and transform or eradicate.

My own experiences with lucid dreaming are limited. It is a skill that I have only lately began to practise consciously. However, the few big lucid dreams I have had over the years have been remarkable, and all of them have involved travelling out of my body. The first one, which confirmed to me that I was indeed in my energy body, was when I experienced hovering over my sleeping body and looking down on it.

Another one occurred when I asked which decision was the right one when I was at a crossroads in my life:

> *The dream involved being at sea in a storm, on a big vessel that had lost its captain. I was required to steer the ship, which of course I didn't have a clue how to do. The moment the ship was keeling over and it became clear that we would all die, I suddenly realized that I was dreaming and could change the dream.*

To cut a long dream short, I changed the setting of the steering wheel to 'automatic' and the ship steered itself. Once I had done this, a voice said: 'It is only when you take responsibility that you will find out that the ship of life steers itself.'

A profound short lucid dream happened during my time in Ecuador with an elder shaman. In accordance with the tradition, he always asked for dreams to be shared in the morning, but rarely offered an interpretation.

In this dream I found myself flying through space, which I enjoyed tremendously. At one point I became very thirsty. All that was on offer, though (from a hand belonging to a translucent woman with red eyes), was a glass of milk. I don't like drinking milk at the best of times and in the dream I consequently refused to take the drink until I could refuse no more because my thirst had become unbearable. I finally took the glass and drank reluctantly.

When I shared the dream, the shaman looked at me and said, quite matter-of-factly, the following, which was translated for me from Quechua into English: 'Milk for you represents the blood of the shaman, the very power that is in your blood. When it is given to you by your ancestor, you refuse to take it. But when the thirst becomes unbearable, you have only two choices: you take your power or you die.'

I remember staring at him rather spellbound. He was so very right. I had always been a reluctant shamanic apprentice and was still very unwilling to be that which was in my very blood. I also knew that you had to follow your calling, as everything else would lead to soul starvation and to a slow inner dying, but I obviously needed to have it spelled out.

Whatever you believe you can do within lucid dreaming, and whatever level you reach, you can learn and practise the skill,[6] and it is a worthwhile undertaking. You can meet spirit guides and teachers and receive instruction, you can learn how to work energetically in the dream state to manifest healing and change; you can begin to understand the journey your soul undertakes when leaving the body and more.

Working within dreams is a skill that, from a shamanic perspective, can only be acquired with a teacher. There are schools that teach how to work within the dream state, but, as with everything, don't expect 'a quick fix'. As with all deeper teachings and tools, caution is also advised, as there are teachers who cannot teach you more than self-hypnotic techniques to achieve lucidity (which is the lowest level). But there are also those whose teachings are based on solid, long-standing systems, whose own experience in this area is outstanding and who have a vast knowledge of dreams and dream work.[7]

The real stuff is profound, although it takes training, perseverance and ethics. If you are interested, or already dream lucidly, this shamanic medicine might be right for you. It will certainly lead you into magical realms, increase your power and help you to be the co-creator of your own life.

Conclusion

The Dreamer and the Dream

This is the right moment to end this book. If you have understood some of the concepts, world-views and practices in shamanism and found your way through the exercises, you will have begun to experience what works for you and what doesn't, what feels connected to your heart and soul and what is not for you – at this moment in time.

You will also have touched the other worlds and some of the forces within them and connected to spirit and spirits. You will already be feeling more integrated and whole and may find that your life is taking a different path, that you are increasingly following your heart's desire and your soul's calling, and that the people who are crossing your path are connected to what you are becoming.

This book has laid the foundation for your shamanic path. If you want to follow it further, you will find teachers – and they will find you – in human form and spirit form. Good human teachers will facilitate your connection to spirit, your awakening and your learning. They will open gateways, hold you if necessary, challenge you when appropriate and assist you in finding your own way, but it is for you to walk it.

On the way, you can access and work with other energetic realities, other worlds, to expand your consciousness, become more connected to the sacred and your soul, and take your place as a co-creator of your own reality and a positive contributor to the manifest reality of the whole that is in a state of Becoming.

We all create reality in the energetic fields. We either do it consciously or we drift through life. I personally don't subscribe to one way of co-creating. There are many ways, and some are more powerful than others, but all are valid. This book has shown you some of them. You co-create when you perform a ceremony, when you drum, when you work with spirit and the sacred, when you use your altar or change one of the stories you have come to believe define you, when you tune into nature, express your wild soul and develop a sense of protectiveness for our environment. You also co-create when you heal and integrate another facet of yourself, when you expand your consciousness, when you work on the level of soul, express your spirit essence, connect with your ancestors or send out a prayer or blessing for our descendants.

When we move forward in our development and gain more power, we change our perception and also the energetic fields, and these changes are reflected back to us and show up in our daily lives as opportunities, coincidences, events and people offering us ways and means to contribute positively to the development of this world.

We are the centre of our own world, but that world enlarges as our perception changes and our consciousness expands. We are both the ocean and the drop and – in some enlightened moments – we perceive both at the same time and understand our true nature.

The shamanic archetype has been awakened in your psyche for a reason. The reason is that humanity's dream is at a critical point and the shamanic can provide an antidote to the disturbing developments in our inner and outer world. You arise from the dream – the cosmic dream as well as the dream humankind has collectively dreamed, which has produced the world we live in. But you are also the dreamer, as you have the power of creation in the energetic fields. Now, more than ever, you are asked, as we are all asked, to examine your dream and dream a better one – one that is in alignment with the sacred Becoming.

> *I wish you magic, connection and love on your journey. I wish for the sacred to enrich your life, for your soul to be nourished and for spirit to support you. Above all, I wish you the joy that arises from finding and walking your very own path with heart and soul on this beautiful planet.*

References and Notes

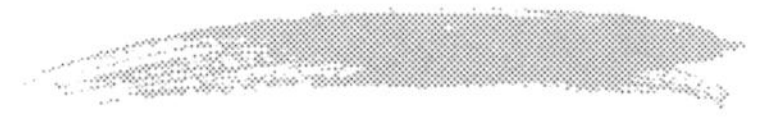

Chapter 1: What is shamanism?

1. C. Pratt, *An Encyclopedia of Shamanism*, Vol. I, The Rosen Publishing Group, Inc., New York, 2007, p.207

2. J. Narby and F. Huxley (eds), *Shamans through Time: 500 Years on the Path of Knowledge*, Thames & Hudson, London, 2001

3. Examples include M. Eliade, *Shamanism: Archaic Techniques of Ecstasy* (Librarie Payot, Paris, 1951; English edition, Princeton University Press, 1964), which surveys shamanism over 2,500 years; and M. Winkelman, 'A cross-cultural study of shamanistic healers' (*Journal of Psychoactive Drugs*, 21, 1989, 17–24), which compares practices in 47 societies, spanning 4,000 years, from 1,750 BC to the present day.

4. J.G. Neihardt, *Black Elk Speaks: Being the Life Story of a Holy Man of the Oglala Sioux*, William Morrow, New York, 1932

5. C. Lévi-Strauss, 'Shamans as Psychoanalysts', 1949, republished in J. Narby and F. Huxley, op. cit.

6. C. Castaneda, *The Teachings of Don Juan: A Yagui Way of Knowledge*, University of California Press, Oakland, California, 1969

7. I have detailed and referenced the research in my previous book, *Shamanism and Spirituality in Therapeutic Practice* (Jessica Kingsley Publishers, 2012).

8. Some of these early western teachers were Brant Secunda, who trained with Matsuwa, a famous Huichol shaman, and founded the Dance of the Deer Foundation; Joan Halifax, the well-known anthropologist and Zen Buddhist, who wrote *Shamanic Voices* (E.P. Dutton and Fitzhenry and Whiteside, 1979) and *Shaman: The Wounded Healer* (Crossroad, 1982); Michael Harner, who established the Foundation for Shamanic Studies, defined 'core shamanism' and spread it widely via his courses; and John Perkins, who studied with the Shuar of the Amazons, the Quechua of the Andes and the Burgis of Indonesia, contributed, with countless books, to a new body of understanding and teaching, and founded the Dream Change Coalition. He took an increasingly critical political and environmental stance, as did Starhawk, Andrew Harvey and others in the shamanic psycho-spiritual activism movement. Alberto Villoldo founded the Four Winds Society, based mainly on Peruvian shamanism, and ran extensive courses, especially in energy healing, whilst Gabrielle Roth based her famous Five Rhythms dance practice on shamanism and the shamanic practitioner Tom Cowan included Celtic shamanism in his work.

9. L. Teish, *Carnival of the Spirit: Seasonal Celebrations and Rites of Passage*, HarperCollins Australia, Sydney, 1994; M.P. Somé, *Of Water and the Spirit: Ritual, Magic and Initiation in the Life of an African Shaman*, G.P. Putnam's Sons, New York, 1994

10. Unfortunately, with Western demand increasing, a number of people pretending to be shamans have appeared in North and South America, offering a variety of hallucinogens, healing ceremonies and teachings, a trend we can now also see for instance in Africa and Mongolia. The same applies to Western teachers and practitioners: there are skilled, experienced, honourable and ethical teachers and there are teachers who will use seekers to feed their own ego. A very good book to read about this subject is Marianna Caplan's *Eyes Wide Open: Practicing Discernment on the Spiritual Path* (Sounds True, Inc., 2009).

Chapter 2: Why shamanism now?

1. Statistics compiled by Oxfam (2014): www.bbc.co.uk/news/business-30875633

2. C.M. Smith, *Jung and Shamanism in Dialogue: Retrieving the Soul/Retrieving the Sacred*, Trafford Publishing, Victoria, BC, 2007

Chapter 3: The shamanic consciousness and world-view

1. The best-publicized research is a study of Buddhist monks, cited in M. Beauregard and D. O'Leary, *The Spiritual Brain*, HarperOne, New York, 2007, pp.71–4. During their meditation practices, Buddhist monks focus their thoughts on loving compassion for all living things. The monks in the study experienced permanent emotional improvement, which was shown through high activity in the left anterior portion of the brain, which is most associated with joy. Additionally, the parts of the brain associated with attention, awareness of sensation, sensory stimuli, and sensory processing were thicker in the meditators than in the controls.

2. What we access depends on our intent, the depth of the state, if we practise entering it repeatedly and become skilled at it, which parts of the brain we deliberately activate and which we deliberately deactivate. It also depends on whether we use psychoactive substances and if we experience very profound brain alteration, such as during an NDE or a traditional shamanic initiation ritual.

3. C.G. Jung, *Symbols of Transformation*, G. Adler and R.F.C. Hull (eds), *Collected Works*, Vol. V, Princeton University Press, Princeton, NJ, 1967

4. I will come back to the dreamworld and dreaming later in this book. Not all of the grandmothers you dream about – to stay with this example – would be seen as spirits, because some of the figures we encounter arise from our personal subconscious –e.g. it could be a memory of your own grandmother.

5. J.G. Neihardt, *Black Elk Speaks*, William Morrow, New York, 1932; annotated edition State University of New York Press, Albany, NY, 2008, p.33

6. M. Pallamary, *Spirit Matters*, Mystic Ink Publications, Carlsbad, CA, 2001

7. M. Eliade, *Shamanism: Archaic Techniques of Ecstasy*, Librarie Payot, Paris, 1951; English edition, Princeton University Press, Princeton, NJ, 1964, pp.35–58

8. P. van Lommel, *Consciousness Beyond Life: The Science of the Near-Death Experience*, HarperOne, New York, 2010

9. If you would like to delve deeper into this subject, I have outlined the developments in quantum physics, field theory and higher mathematics in my previous book and connected them to the shamanic world-view. See C. Mackinnon, *Shamanism and Spirituality in Therapeutic Practice*, Jessica Kingsley Publishers, London, 2012, pp.83–94.

10. Vibrations are repetitive wave-like patterns – 'probability patterns' in contemporary language – in physical systems in the atomic and sub-atomic realm. As far as we know from quantum physics, the universe is a field where everything has an inherent wave-like pattern. These patterns are called quantum waves, or probability waves, as they are relatively stable. That stability determines how probable events are on an atomic level and, of course, on the level that we experience as the physical world.

11. D. Chopra, D. Ford, and M. Williamson, *The Shadow Effect*, HarperCollins, New York, 2010, p.88

12. D. Bohm, *Wholeness and the Implicate Order*, Routledge Classics, London and New York, 2002

13. On the whole, spirits are neutral. Nevertheless, they can either cause harm or be helpful to humans. Interaction with helpful spirits creates greater harmony, improves wellbeing and is a source of wisdom, guidance and power. Interaction with other spirits, such as the spirit of a dead person who hasn't passed over properly to the land of the dead, or a spirit who intrudes into this world using a host's body, can be harmful.

Chapter 4: Shamanic territories

1. The Japanese regard Mount Fuji as the centre of the world, whilst for the Sioux it is the Black Hills of Dakota and in Judaism the Temple Mount in Jerusalem. The famous Mount

Kailash in Tibet serves in this capacity for traditional Hindus, as well as for some streams of Buddhism, where it is seen as the gateway to the mythical land of Shambhala. The Kun-Lun mountain chain in China stands at the centre of the Taoist world. We also have man-made symbols that represent the *axis mundi*: the staff carried by wise men and also used as a symbol in medicine; the pyramids of Teotihuacan in Mexico, with their stairways that lead to the sky; the poles of ascension in Mongolia and Siberia; and man-made hills all over the world.

2. Descriptions of the three worlds are on the whole based on the research of Mircea Eliade (1951/1964) and Michael Harner (1980) (*see Further Reading*), but variations are used worldwide, as well as by most contemporary Western practitioners. There are numerous levels within each of these worlds – in some Toltec traditions, for instance, there are 13 heavens or upper worlds – and details also vary, but not significantly. There is debate as to whether they exist independently of the human mind or are levels of human consciousness. In a strictly shamanic sense, they do exist independently of the human mind but are accessible through it and are therefore also levels of consciousness.

3. S. Ingerman and H. Wesselman, *Awakening to the Spirit World: The Shamanic Path of Direct Revelation*, Sounds True, Inc., Boulder, Colorado, 2010, p.31

Chapter 5: Bringing the shamanic dimension into your daily life

1. C.G. Jung, *Memories, Dreams, Reflections*, Vintage Books, New York, 1961

2. A dreamlodge is a 'place of looking within'. It is different from introspection, as it's a spirit power state and place. It is retreating into a dreaming state to access inner knowing. Traditionally, it was done communally in a lodge. Women did it during their menses.

3. Don Martin Pinedo, shaman/healer of a lineage of shamans from Peru, in *Shaman's Drum*, Vol. 89. *Shaman's Drum* was a journal of the Cross-Cultural Shamanism Network. It ceased

publication in 2013. Back copies can be requested from the Shaman's Drum Foundation, www.shamansdrumfoundation.org

Chapter 6: The shamanic journey

1. M. Harner, *The Way of the Shaman: A Guide to Power and Healing*, Harper & Row, New York, 1980

2. S. Ingerman, *Shamanic Journeying: A Beginner's Guide*, Sounds True, Boulder, Colorado, 2004

3. C. Pratt, *An Encyclopedia of Shamanism*, The Rosen Publishing Group, Inc., New York, 2007, p.25

Chapter 8: The power and beauty of ceremony and ritual

1. M.P. Somé, *Of Water and the Spirit: Magic and Initiation in the Life of an African Shaman*, Penguin, New York, 1994, p.32

2. E.L. Rossi, *A Discourse with our Genes: The Psychosocial and Cultural Genomics of Therapeutic Hypnosis and Psychotherapy*, Editris S.A.S., Benevento, 2004. Provides a good overview over the research into holistic brain responses.

3. S. Somé, *The Spirit of Intimacy: Ancient Teachings in the Ways of Relationships*, William Morrow, New York, 1999

4. R. Walsh, MD, PhD, *The World of Shamanism: New Views of an Ancient Tradition*, Llewellyn Publications, Woodbury, Minnesota, 2007

5. If you are interested in a detailed descriptions of the traditional ways of using ceremonies, including the fire ceremony, you will find them in my previous book, *Shamanism and Spirituality in Therapeutic Practice* (Jessica Kingsley Publishers, 2012).

Chapter 9: Dancing with spirit

1. G. Roth, *Sweat your Prayers: Movement as Spiritual Practice*, Penguin Putnam, New York, 1998, p.6. (The expression 'the wrong garden', referring to the Garden of Eden, is used to describe the arrival of Judaism, Christianity and Islam.)

2. The traditional Sun Dance of the tribes of the Great Plains in North America is just one example of dance being used to achieve profound altered states of consciousness, to connect with spirit, to initiate, to honour the sun and to bring vision and medicine power to the dancers. Traditionally the Sun Dance lasted for three to four days, with a period of fasting, cleansing and praying beforehand and continuous fasting during the period of the dance. Dancers went on until they lost consciousness, often reporting spirit walks and visions during the ceremonies and celebrations. Each dancer's intent was their own, and their journey during the dance and their encounters with spirits and powers were theirs to manage and endure, but the medicine power they gained was to serve the family and the community.

3. N. Frank, *Trance Dance: The Dance of Life*, Element Books, Shaftesbury, 1995. Provides a good overview of indigenous trance dance practices.

4. http://tinyurl.com/pf8ae4p

5. J. Verghese, R.B. Lipton, M.J. Katz, C.B. Hall, G. Kuslansky, C.A. Derby, A.F. Ambrose, M. Sliwinski, H. Buschke, 'Leisure activities and the risk of dementia in the elderly', *New England Journal of Medicine* 2003, Vol. 348, pp.2, 508–516

Chapter 10: The medicine wheel

1. Wheel interpretations, such as the teachings of the different directions, differ slightly from region to region and there also are adaptations by contemporary shamanic practitioners. I have been taught a combination of the Hopi and Mayan wheel and will use this here. For the purpose of this book I will only include some nature aspects of the four directions as well as basic human aspects. If you are interested in exploring the medicine wheel further, I have included eight directions and a split centre – 10 aspects – in my previous book, *Shamanism and Spirituality in Therapeutic Practice* (Jessica Kingsley Publishers, 2012), and also explained in more detail how the wheel works when taking more directions into account. There are also some good books that go deep into the medicine wheel, which I have listed in the Further Reading section.

2. Bill Plotkin offers a new, very insightful approach in his book *Nature and the Human Soul: Cultivating Wholeness and Community in a Fragmented World* (New World Library, 2008), using the wheel to describe the eight stages of human development, personal, social and spiritual, and defining the tasks at each stage to become 'who we can be', based on the hero's journey and spiritual development.

3. If you are interested in learning a bit more about the medicine wheel, see my previous book, *Shamanism and Spirituality in Therapeutic Practice* (Jessica Kingsley Publishers, 2012).

Chapter 11: Spirit, soul and the sacred in nature

1. M.R. Ungunmerr-Bauman, *Dadirri:* Inner Deep Listening and Quiet Still Awareness, http://tinyurl.com/qbbbabl, 2007

2. Quoted in J. Narby, *The Cosmic Serpent: DNA and the Origins of Knowledge*, Georg Editeur, Geneva, 1995; English translation Victor Gollancz, London, 1998; second impression Jeremy P. Tarcher, New York, 2003, p.24

3. E. Gatoga, www.freepressjournal.in/the-call-of-nature/

4. Genesis 1:28

5. http://tinyurl.com/oal58an

6. O. Lyons, www.indigenouspeople.net/orenlyon.htm, p.1

7. Details about research into the connection between nature and human wellbeing can be found in my book *Shamanism and Spirituality in Therapeutic Practice* (Jessica Kingsley Publishers, 2012), pp.263–5.

8. B. Plotkin, *Nature and the Human Soul: Cultivating Wholeness and Community in a Fragmented World*, New World Library, Novato, California, 2008, p.6

Chapter 12: Embedded in the cycle of life

1. Generation after generation has been introduced to archetypal teachings and figures via fairy tales, which has allowed them to

immerse themselves in a world beyond their ordinary reality, identify with the trials and tribulations of the characters, and, in the process, learn about the cycles of fear and overcoming fear, of tension and release, and of fighting evil so that good could triumph. The latest example, in the form of the phenomenal worldwide success of the Harry Potter books and films, has proved again the amazing impact of well-constructed stories centred on the magical and archetypal.

2. I am restricting myself to the creation story. But many of the stories we tell ourselves are restrictive. I have written more extensively about how we can become aware of such stories and change them in a shamanic/therapeutic context in my previous book, *Shamanism and Spirituality in Therapeutic Practice* (Jessica Kingsley Publishers, 2012).

3. C. Pratt, *An Encyclopedia of Shamanism*, Vol. II, The Rosen Publishing Group, Inc., New York, 2007, p.14

4. Due to the breathtakingly fast industrial and military developments of the last few centuries, and especially the devastating wars, the religious crusades, the slavery, imperialism, fascism and other 'isms', as well as the devastating ecological consequences of our recent way of life (to name but a few), we may not find many wise teachers in our recent ancestry. On the whole, our more recent ancestors didn't live lives that were, in a traditional sense, healthy, good or wholesome, as they didn't live lives in accordance with spirit. They therefore have less wisdom than the ancestors who lived Earth-based lives.

5. O. Lyons, 'An Iroquois Perspective' in *American Indian Environments: Ecological Issues in Native American History*, C. Vecsey and R.W. Venables (eds), Syracuse University Press, New York, 1980, pp.173–4

6. B. Plotkin, *Nature and the Human Soul: Cultivating Wholeness and Community in a Fragmented World*, New World Library, Novato, California, 2008, p.201

7. Psychopomps are shamans who stay with the dying and lead their souls into the other realms. They also work with souls who get stuck between the worlds, as can happen when we

die a sudden, violent or traumatic death. The big wars that have characterized the last few millennia have produced, according to certain strands of shamanism, vast energy fields that are 'contaminated' with such stuck souls.

8. Eve Bruce, a surgeon from the USA, includes her experiences with the same shamanic initiation ritual in more detail in her book *Shaman MD* (Destiny Books, Rochester, Vermont, 2002).

Chapter 13: Sacred medicine plants

1. M. Pallamary, *Spirit Matters*, Mystic Ink Publishing, Carlsbad, CA, 2007, p.154

2. There is an increasingly fascinating body of research into the psychological and therapeutic applications of psychedelics, their workings on the brain and how they enhance personality and consciousness within the academic fields of psychology and neuroscience. In the UK, Prof. David Nutt, Prof. Roland Hopkins, Dr David Luke and Dr Amanda Fielding are some of the better-known researchers involved.

3. I have described the Gabonese healing ritual with ibogaine in depth, including the 'scientific' interpretations of how what happens in the brain, in my previous book, *Shamanism and Spirituality in Therapeutic Practice* (Jessica Kingsley Publishers, 2012), pp.104–109.

4. Lesley Myburgh, www.shamanicretreats.org/san-pedro/

5. R.G. Wasson, 'Seeking the magic mushroom', *Life* magazine, June 10, 1957, reproduced www.imaginaria.org/wasson/life.html, 2011

6. If you are interested, Terrence McKenna's books (*see Further Reading*) and videos offer a wealth of experiences, information and discussions about the subject: www.ayahuascacommunity.com/terrence-mckenna/

7. Pallamary, op. cit.

Chapter 14: Shamanic work in the dreamworld

1. R. Anwander, The International Association for the Study of Dreams (IASD), 'Dreams without Borders' conference, Montreal, Quebec, 2008. Stanley Kippner also describes these dream practices on his website: http://stanleykrippner.weebly.com.

2. S. Magaña, *The Toltec Secret: Dreaming Practices of the Ancient Mexicans*, Hay House, London, 2014

3. L. Irwin, *The Dream Seekers: Native American Visionary Traditions of the Great Plains*, University of Oklahoma Press, Norman, Oklahoma, 1996, p.237

4. R. Modesto, and G. Mount, *Not for Innocent Ears: Spiritual Traditions of a Desert Cahuilla Medicine Woman*, Sweetlight Books, California, 1986; second edition 1989, p.6

5. S.M.S. Jones and S. Krippner, *The Voice of Rolling Thunder: A Medicine Man's Wisdom for Walking the Red Road*, Bear & Company, Rochester, Vermont, 2012

6. Stanley Krippner is an outstanding professor of psychology and eminent researcher. His publications reach into the hundreds, including around 30 books, and he is one of the leading experts on shamanic dream practices. His website, http://stanleykrippner.weebly.com, provides a wealth of information on dreaming and other shamanic subjects.

7. For example, Sergio Magaña. See *The Toltec Secret*, op. cit.

Further Reading

Classics and overviews

Mircea Eliade, *Shamanism: Archaic Techniques of Ecstasy*, Librarie Payot, Paris, 1951; English edition, Princeton University Press, 1964

Michael Harner, *The Way of the Shaman: A Guide to Power and Healing*, Harper & Row, 1980

Christa Mackinnon, *Shamanism and Spirituality in Therapeutic Practice*, Jessica Kingsley Publishers, London, 2012

John G. Neihardt, *Black Elk Speaks: Being the Life Story of a Holy Man of the Oglala Sioux*, William Morrow, New York, 1932; annotated edition State University of New York Press, Albany, NY, 2008

Christina Pratt, *An Encyclopedia of Shamanism*, Vols I & II, The Rosen Publishing Group, Inc., New York, 2006, 2007

Roger Walsh, MD, PhD, *The World of Shamanism: New Views of an Ancient Tradition*, Llewellyn Publications, Woodbury, Minnesota, 2007

World regions

Tom Cowan, *Fire in the Head: Shamanism and the Celtic Spirit*, HarperCollins*Publishers*, 1993

Sidian Morning Star Jones and Stanley Krippner, *The Voice of Rolling Thunder: A Medicine Man's Wisdom for Walking the Red Road*, Bear & Company, Rochester, Vermont, 2012

Sarangerel Odigan, *Riding Windhorses: A Journey into the Heart of Mongolian Shamanism*, Destiny Books, Rochester, Vermont, 2000

Malidoma Patrice Somé, *The Healing Wisdom of Africa: Finding Life Purpose through Nature, Ritual and Community*, Jeremy P. Tarcher, New York, 1999

Journeying

Sandra Ingerman, *Shamanic Journeying: A Beginner's Guide*, Sounds True, Boulder, Colorado, 2004

Alberto Villoldo, PhD, *Mending the Past and Healing the Future with Soul Retrieval*, Hay House, 2005

Dance and drumming

Michael Drake, *The Shamanic Drum: A Guide to Sacred Drumming*, Talking Drum Publications, Salem, Oregon, 2002, revised edition 2009

Susannah and Ya'Acov Darling Khan, *Movement Medicine: How to Awaken, Dance and Live Your Dreams*, Hay House, London, 2009

Gabrielle Roth, *Sweat your Prayers: Movement as Spiritual Practice*, Jeremy P. Tarcher, New York, 1997

The medicine wheel

Jamie Sams, *Dancing the Dream: The Seven Sacred Paths to Human Transformation*, HarperSanFrancisco, 1999

Sun Bear and Wabun, *The Medicine Wheel: Earth Astrology*, Prentice Hall, 1980

Nature

Ted Andrews, *Nature Speaks: Signs, Omens and Messages in Nature*, Dragonhawk Publishing, Jackson, Tennessee, 2004

Bill Plotkin, *Nature and the Human Soul: Cultivating Wholeness and Community in a Fragmented World*, New World Library, Novato, California, 2008

Plant medicine/consciousness

Graham Hancock (ed.), *The Divine Spark: Psychedelics, Consciousness and the Birth of Civilisation*, Hay House, London, 2015

Terrence McKenna, *Food of the Gods: The Search for the Original Tree of Knowledge: A Radical History of Plants, Drugs and Human Evolution*, Bantam Books, New York, 1992

Terrence McKenna: A very good collection of his talks and interviews can be found at: www.ayahuascacommunity.com/terrence-mckenna/

Ralph Metzner, PhD (ed.), *The Ayahuasca Experience: A Sourcebook on the Sacred Vine of Spirits*, Park Street Press, Rochester, Vermont, 2014 (first published as *Ayahuasca: Human Consciousness and the Spirits of*

Nature, Thunder's Mouth Press, 1999; reissued as *Sacred Vine of Spirits: Ayahuasca*, Park Street Press, 2006)

Daniel Pinchbeck, *Breaking Open the Head: A Psychedelic Journey into the Heart of Contemporary Shamanism*, Broadway Books, New York, 2002

Dreaming

Sergio Magaña, *The Toltec Secret: Dreaming Practices of the Ancient Mexicans*, Hay House, London, 2014

Stanley Kippner is one of the leading experts on shamanic dream practices. His website is: http://stanleykrippner.weebly.com.

Index

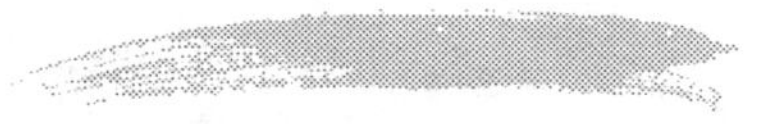

A

Aboriginals 9, 90, 115, 175, 178
African shamanism 3, 4, 9, 23, 90, 91, 92, 97, 106, 107, 146, 156, 165–6
Alix, Wilbert 108–9
alpha brainwaves/state 18, 37
altars 48–51, 74, 95, 145
altered states of consciousness/perception 10, 44–5
  accessing material from personal subconscious 19
  accessing transpersonal realms 19–20
  and the brain 17–19
  ecstatic states *see* ecstasy
  extreme visionary states 21–4
  through ceremony 92, 96
  through dance *see* dance
  through hallucinogens *see* hallucinogens
  trance *see* trance
Alzheimer's disease 109
Amazon 4, 9
Americas 3, 4, 8, 9, 90, 96, 97, 107, 115, 127, 156
ancestral spirits 8, 29, 47
  connecting with 146–9
Andes 4, 9
animal spirits 8, 29, 46, 67, 71, 127, 142, 165
  power animals *see* power animals
animals, slaughtering and eating 127
anxiety disorders 14, 15
archetypes
  archetypal symbolism 11, 20
  and myths 141–2
  shamanic archetype xv–xvi, 13–14, 15, 187
  spirits as 20
Australia 3
  Aboriginals 9, 90, 115, 175, 178
autumn equinox 100
axis mundi 31–2
ayahuasca 163, 169–71

B

Balinese masked dancing 106
beauty
  and the altar 50
  of ceremony and ritual 93–4
  infusing space with 52–3
Becoming, state of 27–8, 186, 187
  great web of Being and Becoming 134
beta brainwaves/state 18, 37

Big Bang theory 26
Black Elk 6, 22, 27, 179–80
Bodhi tree 32
Bohm, David 27
brain 17–19
  neural gateways opened by plant teachers 161
  scanning 18
  waves and states 18, 20, 21, 37, 38, 44, 61
Brazil xvii, 106, 178
breathing techniques 110
Buddha 32
Buddhism 57, 97
Buryat tribe 23

C

Castaneda, Carlos 167
  The Teachings of Don Juan 6
cave paintings 3
celebration 102
ceremonial space 57, 90, 93, 95, 101, 109, 115
ceremonies *see* rituals/ceremonies
chakra dancing 112–13
Cheltuev, Slava 128
Chopra, Deepak 26
cleansing of space 52–3, 95
clothing 8
collective unconscious 19–20
consciousness
  altered states of *see* altered states of consciousness/perception
  awareness walks 131, 137–8
  becoming conscious of the gifts of nature 132
  and the brain 17–19
  joy of pure consciousness 143
  movement 9
  pool of 25, 141
  shamanic 17–24 *see also* altered states of consciousness/perception
  sleep state 176 *see also* dream work
  striving for expansion of 38, 151, 186
  and the three cosmic worlds 32–6
  travelling whilst body is clinically dead 23–4
  see also perception
cosmic dream 187
cosmic tree 32, 34
cosmology
  and ancestors *see* ancestral spirits
  axis mundi 31–2
  consciousness and the three cosmic worlds 32–6
  consciousness movement's incorporation of shamanic cosmology 9
  creation myths 141–6
  and descendants 149–51
  earth-based traditional 125–9
    see also nature
  interconnectedness *see* interconnectedness
  lower world 33–4
  middle world 35–6
  shamanic territories 31–6
  upper world 34–5
creation myths 141–6

D

Dagara people 9
dance
  Balinese masked dancing 106
  chakra dancing 112–13
  contemporary adaptations 108–14
  dancing the journey 105–12, 158–9
  dancing with spirit 105–14
  with drumming 106, 107
  ecstatic/trance dances 8, 11, 90–91, 105–12

'expressing my rainbow self' 86–7
Five Rhythms wave dancing 111–12
ghost dances 106
of gratitude 86
healing through 86, 108–9, 159
and health 108–9
integration through 85–7, 114
your last dance 158–9
to 'let go of control' 86
merging through 114
peyote dances 106, 107
with a 'retrieved part' 85–6
with singing 107
sun dances 90, 106
traditional trance dance 105–7
voodoo trance dances 106
whirling 106, 110
death 151–9
and dismemberment xvii, 21, 23, 153
and the gifts we receive 152–4
shamanic working with 154–9
delta brainwaves/state 18, 21, 38
depression 14, 15
descendants, connecting with 149–51
disenchantment 129
dismemberment xvii, 21, 23, 153
divination 72, 89, 100, 107, 162
see also prophecy
dream work 175–83
arising from the dream 187
and healing 177
intentional dreaming 177, 179–83
lucid dreaming 177, 179–83
normal dreaming and sharing 178
prophetic dreams 177, 178, 179–80, 181
drumming 8, 44, 45–6, 61, 63
with dance 106, 107
download 63, 65, 70, 74, 77, 113, 158
with plant medicine 162

E
Eagle 37, 68
Earth balance 91
ecstasy 162, 171
shamans as 'masters' of 6
Ecuador xvii, 169, 178, 182
Shuar tribe 178
electroencephalography (EEG) 18
elements, four 50, 116
Eliade, Mircea: *Shamanism* 6
embodiment
of energy in power objects 50, 56–9
through dance 114
energy
body 20, 23 *see also* consciousness; souls
and dance 108–9
depletion 15, 28
developing trust when working with energies 45
directed by intent 42–3
embodiment in power objects 50, 56–9
energy healing 11
fields 22, 25, 35, 36, 93, 186
psychology 25
re-energizing 49, 130–31
sealing 51
spirits as energetic entities 29
see also spirit/spirit allies
environmental devastation 14
ethno-medicine 9
Evenki language 4

F
fire breath 110
fire ceremony 90, 96–7, 101–2, 149
formation myths 141–6

functioning magnetic resonance imaging (fMRI) scans 18

G

Gabonese ceremonies 91
Gatoga, Eli 128
ghost dances 106
Great Spirit 26
Guarani tribe 178
guidance 34–5, 53, 62, 66, 69, 75, 82, 118, 164
  spirit guides/teachers 29, 35, 71–4, 148

H

Haiti 106
hallucinogens
  peyote dances 106, 107
  psychoactive sacred plants 8, 22, 23–4, 106, 107, 161–73
Harner, Michael 61
healing
  ceremonies 35–6, 90, 96, 162–73
  in contemporary shamanism 10
  and dance 86, 108–9, 159
  with dream work 177
  energy healing approaches 11
  Gabonese 91
  in the middle world 35
  nature's healing power 129–30
  physical 81–3
  plant medicine ceremonies 90, 162–73
  psycho-spiritual work between the worlds 75–88
  in traditional shamanism 5
herbs 8
higher/true self 35, 62, 178
Hopi people 8
Huichol people 106, 107, 167
Hummingbird 37

I

ibogaine 165–6
inequalities 14
Ingerman, Sandra 34, 61
initiation practices 22
  dismemberment xvii, 21, 23, 153
  facing death 155–7, 159
  Gabonese 91
integration work
  with ancestors 148–9
  with your creation story 145–6
  into daily life 41–59, 145–6
  with descendants 150–51
  with journeys 85–8
  into other movements and practices xviii–xix, 9
  with power animals 71
  with spirits 71, 74
  with your teacher 74
  through dance 85–7, 114
  through objects or paintings 87–8
intent 42–3
  ceremony as enactment of 89, 92, 94, 96, 99 *see also* rituals/ceremonies
  dreaming with 177, 179–83
  embodied through dance 114
  planting intentions 102
  and shamanic journeys 76, 78, 80, 81
interconnectedness 25, 126–9
  connecting with ancestors 146–9
  connecting with descendants 149–51
  connecting with spirit 53–6, 66–74, 135, 136–8
  embedment in the cycle of life 141–59
  and integration *see* integration work
  and interdependence 7
  meeting and connecting with power animals 66–71

reconnecting with the sacred in nature and your own nature 131–8
interdependence 7
international Indigenous Leadership Gathering (2014) 128
Inuit people 106
Iroquois cosmic tree 32
Irwin, Lee 178
isolation 14

J
Jaguar 37
journeys, shamanic 61–74
to connect with ancestors 148
to connect with descendants 150
dancing the journey 105–12, 158–9 *see also* dance
in dreams *see* dream work
establishing your place of power 64–6
facing death 157–9
integration of 85–8
and intent 76, 78, 80, 81
lower world 33–4, 66–71, 75
middle world 35–6
out-of-body experiences 21–4
for physical healing 81–3
plant journeys 90, 162–5, 168–9, 170–71
preparation 77
and psycho-spiritual work between the worlds 75–88
of release 79–81
of retrieval 77–9
skills and means for 7–8
structure of 63–4
traditional and contemporary journeying 62–3
transformative 77–85
upper world 34–5, 71–4, 75, 144–5
Jung, Carl Gustav 20, 42

K
Kabir 27
karma 28
Kogi people 91
Krippner, Stanley 180

L
Lakota people 8
sun dance ceremony 90
Lévi-Strauss, Claude 6
life-force 25–6, 28
see also spirit/spirit allies
listening, deep 43–4, 58, 131, 136
Lommel, Pim van 24
loneliness 14
lower world 33–4
shamanic journeys and work 33–4, 66–71, 75
spirits 34, 66–71 *see also* power animals
lucid dreaming 179–83
Lyons, Oren R. 128–9, 149

M
Magaña, Sergio: *The Toltec Secret* 178
Manchu tribe 23
mandalas 57, 115
manifestation 87–8, 93, 96
Maori traditions 115
Mapuche tribe 178
Mara'akames 91
materialism 14
medicine wheels 11, 115–24
the circle 122–3
diagonals 123–4
exercises 118–19, 120–21
going deeper 121–2
human aspects 119–20
and the power of the four directions 116–19, 121–2
meditation 44, 131
and the brain 18
mental illness
refutation that shamans are mentally ill 6

during shamanic initiation 7
and the 'soulless' society 14–15
merging 114, 131
mescaline 166, 167
Mexican shamans xvii, 8, 9, 90, 91, 167
Huichol people 106, 107, 167
middle world 35–6
shamanic journeys and work 35–6
spirits 35
Modesto, Ruby 180
Mongolian shamanism 4, 9, 23, 32, 97, 106, 107
moon ceremonies 99, 102–3
Morris, William 53
mushrooms 167–9
Myburgh, Lesley 166
myth 11, 33
and archetypes 141–2
power of formation myths 141–6

N

nature
awareness walks 131, 137–8
becoming conscious of the gifts of 132
being seen by Mother Nature 132–3
contemporary shamanic nature work and tools 130–38
earth-based traditional cosmology 125–9
healing power of 129–30
human 'separation' from 126, 129–30
reconnecting with the sacred in nature and your own nature 131–8
the sacred in 125–38
spirits 8, 29, 35, 41, 75, 101, 126, 130
Navajo people 8
Kinaalda ritual 90
near-death experiences (NDEs) 17, 18, 24, 153
see also dismemberment
Neihardt, John 6
Nepal 9, 106
New Zealand 3, 115
Maori traditions 115

O

Oneness 26
Orang Aoli people 178
Ostyak tribe 23
out-of-body experiences 21–4

P

Pallamary, Matthew 22–3, 164
perception
altered states of *see* altered states of consciousness/perception
and the brain 17–19
four levels of human perception 36–8
Peru xvii, 169
peyote 167
dances 106, 107
pilgrimage 91
Pinedo, Martin 51
plants
peyote dances 106, 107
plant medicine ceremonies 90, 162–73
sacred psychoactive medicine/teacher plants 8, 22, 23–4, 106, 107, 9161–73
Plotkin, Bill 129
possession, spirit 91, 106, 107
power animals 34, 114
integration of 71
meeting and connecting with 66–71
power objects 50, 56–9
power places 64–6
power tools 8
prayer flags 97
prophecy 107, 162
prophetic dreams 177, 178, 179–80, 181

psycho-spiritual work, between the worlds 75–88
psychoactive sacred plants 8, 22, 23–4, 106, 107, 161–73

Q

quantum realm 25

R

rattling 45–6, 162
reality 29
  energetic/non-ordinary realities 33 *see also* lower world; upper world
  of spirit worlds 45
receptivity 43–4
release
  ceremonies 96, 101
  journeys of 79–81
  of objects 87
retrieval
  dancing with a 'retrieved part' 85–6
  journeys of 77–9
  soul-retrieval stones 49, 59
retuning 96
rituals/ceremonies
  and altered states 92, 96
  ancestor ceremonies 149
  and beauty 93–4
  ceremonial space 57, 90, 93, 95, 101, 109, 115
  in contemporary shamanism 11
  creating an altar 48–51, 95
  creating your own ceremony 94–103
  and the creation of harmony 90, 92, 93–4
  daily ritual to connect with spirit 53–6
  diverse uses of 89
  enactment of intent through 89, 92, 94, 96, 99
  ending 95
  evening 55–6
  for facing death 155–9
  fire ceremony 90, 96–7, 101–2, 149
  of healing 35–6, 90, 96, 162–73
  holistic responses as ceremony works its magic 92–4
  honouring the spirit of place and your own place 133–4
  initiation *see* initiation practices
  moon ceremonies 99, 102–3
  morning 53–5
  on pilgrimage 91
  plant medicine ceremonies 90, 162–73
  power and beauty of 89–103
  preparation 96
  of release 96, 101
  ritualized dances 107 *see also* dance
  seasonal 99–102
  structuring a basic ceremony 94–5
  traditional 8, 90–91
  tree ceremony 97–9, 149
rock art 3
Rolling Thunder 180–81
Roth, Gabrielle 105, 111–12
Russia 3

S

sacredness xv, xviii, xx, 10, 22
  altars 48–51
  everything as sacred and evolving 27
  infusing space with the sacred 52–3
  modern deprivation of 13
  in nature 125–36
  of original Source 26
  reconnecting with the sacred in nature and your own nature 131–8

sacred medicine plants 8, 22, 23–4, 106, 107, 161–73
sense of the sacred 48
and the shamanic archetype 15
starving of our sacred Earth souls 129–30
Salish spirit dance 106
San Pedro cactus 166
Sanchez, Victor 156
seasonal ceremonies 99–102
self, higher/true 35, 62, 178
Serpent 36–7
shadows 33
shamanic archetype 13–14, 15, 187
surfacing into consciousness xv–xvi
shamanic callings xvii, 185
shamanic consciousness 17–24
see also altered states of consciousness/perception
shamanic path and practices
basic skills and tools 42–6
ceremonies *see* rituals/ceremonies
characteristics of contemporary shamanism 10–11
characteristics of traditional shamanism 7–8
Christian antipathy 5
contemporary Western practice and revival of interest 8–11
cosmology underlying *see* cosmology
and death *see* death
shamanic path and practices
divination *see* divination
dream work *see* dream work
Far Eastern 3, 9, 96
global extent 3–4, 5
healing *see* healing
historical accounts 5
historical roots and development 3–4
initiation *see* initiation practices
integration work *see* integration work
and interconnectedness *see* interconnectedness
journeys *see* journeys, shamanic
meaning and nature of shamanism 3–11
and nature *see* nature
present popularity 13–15
prophetic *see* prophecy
psycho-spiritual work, between the worlds 75–88
of retrieval *see* retrieval
rituals *see* rituals/ceremonies
and the sacred *see* sacredness
with spirits *see* spirit/spirit allies
twentieth-century studies 5–6
and the way forward 185–7
world-view of 24–9
shamans
African 3, 4, 9, 23, 90, 91, 92, 97, 106, 107, 146, 156, 165–6
bridging energetic and material worlds xvi, 7–8, 10 *see also* interconnectedness
dancing *see* dance
dismemberment xvii, 21, 23, 153
European accusations against 5
experienced shaman/guides 157, 163, 164, 172
initiation *see* initiation practices
integration work *see* integration work
journeys *see* journeys, shamanic
as 'masters of ecstasy' 6
Mexican *see* Mexican shamans
Mongolian 9, 23, 32, 97, 106, 107

names for 4, 175
nature work and tools 130–38
and psychoanalysts 6
scope of work 6, 10–11
Siberian 9, 32, 106, 107
South American practitioners and practices 4, 8, 90, 96, 97, 107, 115, 127, 156
and spirits *see* spirit/spirit allies
training 7, 21–2
Western shamanic practitioners 10–11
shapeshifting 8, 91
Shiva 106
Shuar tribe 178
Shuma, Carlos Perez 126–7
Siberian shamanism 4, 9, 32, 106
singing 107
Sioux 106
smoke 8
Somé, Malidoma 9
soul-retrieval stones 49, 59
souls
nourishing the soul 15
soul level of perception 37
'soulless' societies 14
and spirit 28
split-off soul parts 33
starving of our sacred Earth souls 129–30
suffering of the soul 14–15
trapped in middle world 36
South American 4, 8, 90, 96, 97, 107, 115, 127, 156
space
ceremonial 57, 90, 93, 95, 101, 109, 115
cleansing 52–3, 95
infusing with the sacred 52–3
spirit/spirit allies
ancestral spirits *see* ancestral spirits
animal spirits *see* animal spirits
as archetypes 20
calling spirit 46–7, 95
connecting with 53–6, 66–74, 135, 136–8
containers of spirit 51
dancing with spirit 105–14
and dismemberment 23
energetic nature of spirits 29
entities experienced with plant medicine 165
extracting a spirit 107
fights with malicious spirits 107
Great Spirit 26
guides/teachers 29, 35, 71–4, 148
hearing the voice of spirit 43–4
honouring the spirit of place and your own place 133–4
integration work with 71, 74
and life-force 25–6
lower world spirits 34, 66–71 *see also* power animals
nature spirits 8, 29, 35, 41, 75, 101, 126, 130
our essence as spirit 27–8
possession 91, 106, 107
power animals *see* power animals
and the soul 28 *see also* souls
spirit level of perception 37–8
spirit of your own place 135
spiritual aspects of all living things 136–8
spiritual field 126, 128
tree spirits 165
working with the help of 11, 29, 33–6, 44–5, 46–7, 72, 156, 157
spirit worlds 7, 19–20, 29, 45
lower *see* lower world
middle *see* middle world
spirit worlds
shamans bridging energetic and material worlds xvi, 7–8, 10 *see also* interconnectedness;

journeys, shamanic
upper *see* upper world
spring equinox 99
stone circles 115, 133
subconscious 130, 142
personal 19
see also collective unconscious
Sufis 106
summer solstice 100–101
sun dances 106
Lakota 90
sweat lodge ceremonies 90, 91, 131

T
teacher plants *see* psychoactive sacred plants
Teish, Luisah: *Carnival of the Spirit* 9
theta brainwaves/state 18, 20, 37, 44, 61
Tibet 9
trance
dance 8, 11, 90–91, 105–12 *see also* dance
movements 8
transpersonal psychology 9
transpersonal realms 19–20
embedment in 93
trees
Bodhi tree 32
cosmic tree 32, 34
spirits of 165
tree ceremony 97–9, 149
trust 45
Tungus tribe 4, 23

U
Umbanda trance dances 106
Ungunmerr-Baumann, Miriam Rose 126
upper world 34–5
shamanic journeys and work 34–5, 71–4, 75, 144–5
spirits 34–5, 71–4

V
vibration 8, 25
instruments/tools of 8, 11, 45–6 *see also* drumming; rattling
spirit as vibrating life-force 25–6
vision quests 91, 131, 147
voodoo trance dances 106

W
walkabout 90
Wasson, Gordon 167
whirling dance 106, 110
winter solstice 100
Wirikuta 167
wisdom 29, 34–5, 66
and ancestral spirits 146, 147
of teacher plants 23, 164
universal 72
Wixaritari 91

Y
Yoruba people 9

ABOUT THE AUTHOR

Christa Mackinnon is a psychologist, family counsellor, clinical hypnotherapist and shamanic practitioner and teacher. She worked internationally for many years as a trauma specialist, therapist, trainer and university lecturer and also spent 10 years as the course director of a large international hypnotherapy training institute.

Her interest in ancient psycho-spiritual traditions and the power of non-ordinary states of consciousness started early in life, mainly influenced by her travels, the writings of C.G. Jung and Carlos Castaneda and her own profound and life-changing spiritual experiences. This led her to learn from and work with Buddhist teachers in Asia, indigenous teachers in the Americas and contemporary shamanic teachers in Europe and the USA.

She has pushed the boundaries of contemporary therapy and psychology by integrating shamanic approaches into her work and is the author of the acclaimed book *Shamanism and Spirituality in Therapeutic Practice*. She writes extensively about the subject in various magazines, speaks at conferences and runs international psycho-spiritual shamanic training courses for therapeutic professionals.

Her renowned workshops and courses for laypeople focus on the various strands of shamanism and mainly take place in Devon, UK, where she now lives with her family.

www.christamackinnon.com

HAY HOUSE

Look within

Join the conversation about latest products,
events, exclusive offers and more.

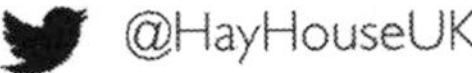

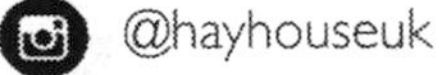

healyourlife.com

We'd love to hear from you!

Printed in the United States
by Baker & Taylor Publisher Services